Company "A" Corps of Engineers, U. S. A.,
1846–1848, in the Mexican War,
by Gustavus Woodson Smith

Company "A" Corps of Engineers, U. S. A., 1846–1848, in the Mexican War, by Gustavus Woodson Smith

Edited by Leonne M. Hudson

THE KENT STATE UNIVERSITY PRESS

Kent, Ohio, and London

© 2001 by The Kent State University Press, Kent, Ohio 44242

All rights reserved.

Library of Congress Catalog Card Number 2001029560

ISBN 0-87338-707-4

Manufactured in the United States of America

05   04   03   02   01   5   4   3   2   1

Library of Congress Cataloging-in-Publication Data

Smith, Gustavus Woodson, 1822–1896.

Company "A" Corps of Engineers, U.S.A., 1846–1848, in the Mexican War /
by Gustavus Woodson Smith ; edited by Leonne M. Hudson

p.   cm.

Includes bibliographical references (p.) and index.

ISBN 0-87338-707-4 (alk. paper) ∞

1. Mexican War, 1846–1848—Engineering and construction. 2. United States.
Army. Corps of Engineers—History—19th century. 3. Mexican War,
1846–1848—Regimental histories—United States. 4. Military engineering—United
States—History—19th century. 5. Smith, Gustavus Woodson,
1822–1896. 6. Mexican War, 1846–1848—Personal narratives, American.
7. Military engineers—United States—Biography.
I. Hudson, Leonne M. II. Title.

E409.2 .S65 2001

973.6'24—dc21   2001029560

British Library Cataloging-in-Publication data are available.

For my mother,
Corine Rhue Hudson
with love and appreciation

Contents

Maps and Illustrations

The company of engineer soldiers, authorized by the act of May 15, 1846, has been more than a year on active duty in Mexico, and has rendered efficient service. I again submit, with approval, the proposition of the Chief Engineer for an increase of this description of force.

Secretary of War to Congress,
Executive Document No. 1, U.S. Senate,
December 7, 1847.

Introduction

More than 150 years ago, the United States and Mexico fought a war that changed both nations forever. Prior to that military event of the middle nineteenth century, the American nation had enjoyed more than three decades of peace with foreign countries. That peace, however, disappeared when the United States declared war on Mexico on May 13, 1846. President James K. Polk, a proponent of expansionism, did not shy away from a fight with his southern neighbor. The diplomatic squabbles between the two countries degenerated into an armed conflict that lasted seventeen months. The patriotism of Americans would be tested as the nation fought a war on foreign soil for the first time in its history.

Two days after the war declaration, Congress passed a bill creating a hundred-man engineer company as part of the regular army. Doubtless, the law satisfied Secretary of War William L. Marcy and Joseph G. Totten, chief engineer of the U.S. Army. Totten had long supported the authorization of such a unit. According to the new legislation, the prospective enlistees of the engineer company had to be American born, physically fit, and of good character. The soldiers had to possess mechanical aptitude and the ability to read and write. The men of the engineer company would be trained at West Point to perform a variety of tasks, including the construction of roads, bridges, batteries, camps, and field fortifications. An important component of their instruction would be infantry tactics. The leadership of the small unit, designated Company A, was entrusted to Alexander J. Swift, Gustavus W. Smith, and George B. McClellan, three talented officers of the Corps of Engineers.[1]

Colonel Totten selected Alexander Swift, the son of Joseph G. Swift, the first graduate of West Point, to command the engineer company. A cadet of impeccable character, he had graduated first in his class of 1830 and was commissioned a brevet second lieutenant in the engineer corps. After leaving the academy, Swift worked constructing forts along the Atlantic coast. In 1838, he was promoted to the rank of captain. Two years later, the War Department sent him to Metz, France, to study at the School of Application for the Artillery and Engineers. Returning to the United States a year later, he joined the West Point faculty as assistant professor of military engineering.[2] Although superb in the field of military science, Swift's education was lacking in the fundamental area of handling troops. This deficiency was due to the adoption of a new infantry drill system in the West Point curriculum after his graduation. Therefore, the task of training the men in infantry maneuvers would fall to Smith and McClellan. Captain Swift was responsible for recruiting enlistees and procuring equipment for the company.

Lieutenant Smith, the ranking officer to Swift, was born in 1822 in Georgetown, Kentucky. Following his education at the local schools on the frontier of the Bluegrass State, he entered West Point in 1838 and graduated four years later, eighth in his class. While there, Smith was keenly aware of the sectional winds blowing across the American landscape. After leaving West Point, he worked on fortification projects in Connecticut. Smith returned to his alma mater in 1844 as assistant professor of engineering. A close friendship developed between Smith and McClellan during the latter's final year at The Point.[3]

The last of the company's leaders was its junior lieutenant, George B. McClellan. He had been born in 1826 in "comfortable surroundings" in Philadelphia. McClellan enjoyed the benefits of preparatory schools and was trained in the classics at a young age. He also attended the University of Pennsylvania, leaving there to enroll at the academy. McClellan was a superb cadet, graduating second in the famous class of 1846. At West Point he gave every indication of becoming "the shining star in the military firmament in the years ahead."[4] In summarizing later the camaraderie of the leaders of the company, Smith would recall that there was "no conflict" among them.

After several weeks of encampment at West Point, the soldiers of Swift's new company were no doubt eager to test their training in the Mexican conflict. According to one source, the seventy-one enlisted men of the company were "well fed, well led, well tuned, and ready for war."[5] Before leaving West Point for the front, a proud Swift rhapsodized in a letter to his father that Company A was a contingent of "fine young men."[6] On September 26, 1846, the engineer company departed from New York with instructions to report to Gen. Zachary Taylor in Mexico. The waterborne journey lasted sixteen days; the unit arrived at Brazos Santiago, on the southern coast of Texas, on October 12.

Once in Mexico, the engineers—also known in those days as "sappers" and "miners"—quickly learned that disease posed a greater threat to their survival than did their adversaries. When the men of Company A pulled out of Matamoros for Victoria on December 21, Swift was left behind to recuperate from dysentery. His illness forced Smith to assume temporary command of the company. Disease so ravaged the company that by the time it reached Victoria, in January 1847, it numbered less than fifty soldiers. They found comfort in knowing that their supervision of road work and bridge building had made it possible for the baggage trains to reach Victoria.

Once there, General Taylor assigned the engineer company to Gen. David E. Twiggs's division, garrisoned at Tampico, 120 miles and a ten-day march away. The men of Company A had significantly improved their engineering skills during their month-long march from Matamoros to Tampico by way of Victoria, a total distance of about 350 miles. After spending a few weeks in Tampico, the engineer company embarked for the port city of Vera Cruz (now Veracruz), on the Gulf coast of Mexico. Upon docking at Anton Lizardo, near Vera Cruz, Smith learned that the company's commander had already arrived from Matamoros.

Though extremely feeble, Captain Swift found the strength to deploy the engineer troops on the beach at Vera Cruz. His participation in the siege of that city in March 1847 was the final effort of his short but brilliant military career. He died of dysentery on April 24 in New Orleans, at the age of thirty-seven. The *New Orleans Commercial Bulletin* memorialized Swift as one who "was eminently gifted with all the most elevated qualities of the soldier and the gentleman."[7] Smith would remember his chief as "one of the best" engineers in the army.

The death of Swift elevated Smith to the position of commanding officer of the engineer company. The Smith-led company was part of General Scott's twelve-thousand-man force that had landed at Vera Cruz on March 9. The execution of that landing had been so precise that not a single casualty was reported. On March 29, the Mexican general, José Juan de Landero, handed over the city to Scott. Following the fall of Vera Cruz, the men of the engineer company began tearing down batteries in preparation to depart from the coast.

They marched out of Vera Cruz on April 13, a journey that would cover 260 miles and end with the capture of Mexico City began. Reaching Plan del Rio four days later, the engineer company became part of Gen. Persifor Smith's brigade, then commanded by Col. William S. Harney. On April 18, Scott's army engaged the Mexicans at Cerro Gordo. In the battle, the sappers and miners proved that they were as handy with muskets as they were with engineering equipment. In his official report, Colonel Harney praised the engineer company for rendering "very efficient service."

With the victory of Cerro Gordo fresh in its men's minds, Company A proceeded to Puebla. There Scott's army set up camp and waited for reinforcements and provisions. The engineer company spent much of its time fortifying the base and drilling. On August 7, the U.S. force left Puebla with the engineer company leading the way through rugged mountains on Scott's approach to the Valley of Mexico. As on previous occasions, the engineer company exhibited a tenacious fighting spirit as an infantry unit at the battles of Contreras and Churubusco in August 1847.

The American army moved deep into the valley. The last bastion protecting the capital city was the fort at Chapultepec; Gustavus

Smith supervised the construction of batteries against that stronghold. The Americans stormed it on September 13 and occupied the Mexican capital the next day. One year after the engineer company left the West Point campus, its military odyssey culminated with a victory celebration in Mexico City. With the exception of occasional skirmishes, the Mexican War was over.

While in the occupied city, Smith's men performed guard duty, inspected battlefields, and drilled. Scott recognized the engineer company as one of the best infantry units in his army, which pleased its commander. Smith, however, was dissatisfied that his force had so few men—less than forty soldiers upon reaching Mexico City. Citing the lack of troops prompted Smith to petition Totten to be relieved from duty with Company A. Colonel Totten honored Smith's request, thus ending his two-year affiliation with the engineer company. Before leaving Mexico City on May 25, Smith turned over command of the company to Lieutenant McClellan. Smith then proceeded to Vera Cruz, where he spent several days attending to financial matters involving the estate of Captain Swift. Sailing from Vera Cruz under its new commander, the engineer company reached West Point on June 22, 1848.

Although the engineer company represented but a fraction of Scott's army, its service was nonetheless valuable during its year-long tour in Mexico. During that time, its men went from inexperienced volunteers to seasoned veterans of several hard-fought battles. In no small measure, the movement of Scott's army depended on the skill and courage of the engineer company. The engineers also made important contributions in the areas of reconnaissance, the selection and preparation of sites for artillery batteries, and supervision of the work of their infantry and artillery comrades. Their combat performance was also notable.

The Mexican campaign provided many graduates of West Point their first real opportunity to test the education and training offered by the Military Academy. Their heroic service convinced lawmakers that West Point was worthy of continued financial support. Mexicans, however, would long view America through lenses of hatred and suspicion. Mexico had lost two-fifths of its territory (including Texas), which increased the size of the United States by approximately one-third. The Mexican cession carried with it seeds of sectional discord. A concomitant of the acquisition of Mexican land was the further polarization of the nation over the extension of slavery into the territories. The Mexican campaigns were, in effect, a dress rehearsal for the Civil War.

Smith and McClellan were representative of the officers who saw action in both wars. They emerged from the Mexican conflict with two brevets each for meritorious service.[8] Although Smith and McClellan would receive high commissions in their respective armies during the early months of the Civil War, neither officer would distinguish himself as a field commander or meet the expectations of their superiors. After the war Smith found employment in the smelting industry, the insurance business, and as an engineer. Another of Smith's major postwar activities should also be noted—writing. After relocating from Kentucky to New York in the late 1870s, he wrote several books and articles. With advanced age his health grew steadily worse, and he died in New York City on June 23, 1896.[9]

Smith's last publication was *Company "A," Corps of Engineers, U.S.A., 1846–'48, in the Mexican War* published by the Battalion Press of New York in 1896. By then, Smith had become a prolific writer. Today, though more than a hundred years old, this well-crafted monograph remains an indispensable treasure for anyone wanting to take a closer look at the engineer company of Mexican War fame. Smith describes how the sappers and miners endured the rigors of combat while performing their many duties. Rich in anecdotal material, this book is a first-person account of the contributions of the only engineer company in the U.S. Army during the war. Smith provides insightful observations of the campaigns in which they participated as an infantry unit.

This volume contains two appendices. Appendix A consists of short excerpts from Cadmus M. Wilcox's *History of the Mexican War* (1892) that essentially highlight Smith's wartime service in Mexico. Appendix B is a roster of the men whom Smith recommended for promotions and appointments in his company.[10] As for sources, Smith relied heavily for quotations on the executive documents collections of the U.S. Senate and the House of Representatives.

My approach to editing Smith's narrative was to maintain the integrity of his work. Although published nearly fifty years after the Mexican War, his recollection of names, dates, places, and military details was remarkably accurate. Brackets are used as they were in the original publication. Smith occasionally used footnotes for explanatory purposes; they have been numbered and converted to endnotes, at the back of the book, for consistency. The term "Smith annotation" has been used to designate citations of Smith's own notes. The editorial, explanatory notes include descriptions of towns, cities, and battles, and give biographical vignettes. The text has been supplemented with photographs, maps, a bibliography, and an index. Smith's text remains as it appeared in 1896. Minor editorial clarifications are enclosed in braces.

I have incurred several debts of gratitude in the process of editing this book. Foremost, I would like to thank my wife, Cassandra, and my son, Evan, for their encouragement, inspiration, and patience as I worked on this volume week after week. Cassandra's mastery of the computer was an invaluable contribution to this endeavor. Her technical knowledge of that piece of equipment kept my frustration to a minimum.

The generous support and assistance of capable individuals at several institutions made my task much easier. I must extend thanks to the staff of the interlibrary-loan office of Kent State University Libraries for their willingness to track down materials for this study. A hearty thanks to Reneé L. Garlock of Audio Visual Services of Kent State University for meticulously and skillfully reproducing the maps in this monograph. I am especially grateful to the Western Reserve Historical Society of Cleveland, Ohio, for providing the photographs of Winfield Scott, Gustavus W. Smith, and George B. McClellan. I would also like to extend sincere thanks to the Department of History at the U.S. Military Academy at West Point for permitting me to reproduce the maps in this volume. Finally, this acknowledgment section would be incomplete without an expression of gratitude to the Special Collections and Archives Division of the U.S. Military Academy for providing the photograph and the papers of Alexander J. Swift.

1

Enlistment, Instruction, Detention on the Rio Grande, March to Victoria and Tampico, Landing at Vera Cruz, Death of Captain Swift

Previous to the war with Mexico there existed among the people of the United States a strong prejudice against maintaining even a small regular army in time of peace. Active opposition to a permanent, regular military establishment extended to the West Point Academy, in which cadets were trained and qualified to become commissioned officers of the army.[1] That Academy was then a component part of the Military Engineer Corps. For years the chief of the Corps had, in vain, urged upon Congress, the necessity for having at least one company of enlisted engineer soldiers as a part of the regular army.

In the meantime he had, however, succeeded in persuading the Government at Washington to send—by permission of the Government of France—a selected Captain of the U.S. Engineer Corps to the French School of engineer officers at Metz; for the purpose of having in the U.S. Army, an officer qualified to instruct and command a company of engineer soldiers in case Congress could be induced to authorize the enlistment of such a company.

Captain Alexander J. Swift was the officer selected to be sent to Metz. On his return to the United States, he was assigned to temporary duty at West Point awaiting the long delayed passage of an act authorizing the enlistment of a company of U.S. Engineer soldiers.

That act was passed soon after the commencement of hostilities with Mexico. It provided for the enlistment of an engineer company of 100 men, in the regular army. The company to be composed of 10 sergeants, 10 corporals, 39 artificers, 39 second class privates, and 2 musicians; all with higher pay than that of enlisted men in the line of the army.

Captain Swift was assigned to the command; and, at his request, I was ordered to report to him as next officer in rank to himself. At my suggestion, Brevet Second Lieutenant George B. McClellan, who had just been graduated from the Military Academy, was assigned as junior officer of the company.

At that time I had been an officer of engineers for four years; my rank was that of second lieutenant. All the first lieutenants, and some of the second lieutenants, of that corps were then in sole charge of the construction of separate fortifications, or were engaged in other important duties. Captain Swift was not disposed to apply for the assignment of any of those officers to be subalterns under him in a company of soldiers.

I had taught McClellan during his last year in the Academy, and felt assured that he would be in full harmony with me in the duties we would be called upon to perform under Captain Swift. It is safe to say that no three officers of a company of soldiers ever worked together with less friction. The understanding between them was complete. There were no jars—no doubts or cross purposes—and no conflict of opinion or of action.

In the beginning I was charged with the instruction of the company as an infantry command, whilst the Captain took control of the recruiting, the collection of engineer implements—including an India Rubber Ponton {pontoon} Bridge—and he privately instructed McClellan and myself, at his own house, in the rudiments of practical military engineering which he had acquired at Metz. In the meantime we taught him, at the same place, the manual of arms and Infantry tactics which had been introduced into the army after he was graduated at the Military Academy. In practical engineer drills the Captain was always in control.

After the men were passably well drilled in the "Infantry School of the Company," the time had come for him to take executive

Alexander J. Swift. Special Collections, USMA Library, West Point

command on the infantry drill ground. He did this on the first oc-casion, like a veteran Captain of Infantry until "at rest" was ordered.

Whilst the men were "at rest," McClellan and myself quietly, but earnestly, congratulated him upon his successful *debut* as drill officer of an Infantry Company. He kindly attributed to our instruction in his house whatever proficiency he had acquired in the new tac-tics which had then been recently introduced.

But, after the company was again called to "Attention" and the drill was progressing, whilst marching with full company front across the plain, the men all well in line, to my surprise the Captain ordered "faster," and added "the step is much too slow." Of course we went "faster." In a short time the Captain ordered "faster still, the step is very much too slow." This order was several times repeated, and before the drill ended we were virtually "at a run."

After the drill was over and the Company dismissed from the parade ground, I asked the Captain why he had not given the commands "quick time" and "double quick," instead of saying "faster" and "still faster." He said he did not intend the step should be "quick time"—much less "double quick." He only wanted the rate to be in "common time—90 steps a minute"; and added: "you had not reached that rate when the drill ended."

I insisted that he must be mistaken, and told him we were marching in "common time" or very near it, when he first gave the order, "faster." He persisted that he was right in regard to the rate of the step—said "that he had carefully counted it, watch in hand"; and added: "You were, at the last, not making more than 85 steps to the minute." I was satisfied that he was mistaken; but he relied implicitly upon the correctness of his count and the accuracy of his watch.

McClellan and I proceeded to the company quarters, of which I still had charge. On the way we referred to the matter of the step, and both of us were at a loss to account for the misapprehension we were sure the Captain labored under in regard to it.

I asked McClellan to take out his watch and count whilst I marched in "common time." I made 90 steps per minute—and repeated it more than once. It presently dawned upon us that our Captain, whilst consulting his watch, had counted only one foot in getting at the number of steps: and that we were really making 170 steps to the minute when he counted 85. The mystery was solved, the Captain had counted "the left foot" only.

When we next went to his house for instruction in details of the school of the engineer soldier, I asked him how many steps we were making a minute when he first ordered "faster." He said "about 45." I replied: "That's it. We have found out what was the matter. You counted only the left foot. We were marching in 'common time' when you ordered us to move 'faster'; and you pushed us to nearly twice that rate."

"The cat was out of the bag." The Captain saw it at once and laughed heartily over the error he had fallen into in the latter part of his "first appearance" as captain, in drilling the company as infantry. He made no such mistake thereafter; and the men never knew of his "count," watch in hand.

On the 26th of September, 1846, we sailed from New York, 71 rank and file, for Brazos Santiago, under orders to report to General Taylor,[2] commanding the U.S. army in Mexico. We landed at Brazos on the 12th of October, remained at that point for several days, proceeded thence to the mouth of the Rio Grande and arrived at Camargo[3] on the 2nd of November. There the company was delayed for several weeks because transportation for the engineer train to the headquarters of the Army at Monterey was not then available.

The Company left Camargo for Brazos on the 29th of November, under orders to proceed to Tampico[4] by sea, but was ordered to return to Matamoros with a portion of its tools, and march, via Victoria,[5] to Tampico—the bulk of its train to be transported to the latter place by water.

Whilst detained at Camargo, instruction in the school of the engineer soldier was kept up, and infantry drills were constantly practiced. During that time several thousand troops were in camp near Camargo, and the men of the engineer company learned that they were, by the line of the army, styled: "the pick and shovel brigade." Their officers advised them not to care for {object to} this epithet but "take it easy, continue to endeavor to become *model* infantry, and engraft on that a fair knowledge of the duties of the engineer soldier." They were assured that "for heavy work," details {teams} would have to be made from the line of the army; and these details would, for the time, constitute the real "pick and shovel brigade" under the control of engineer officers, assisted by trained engineer soldiers. When the time came for close fighting the engineer company would be at the front.

The troops stationed on the Rio Grande during the fall of 1846 suffered greatly from Mexican diarrhea, fevers and other diseases. Several men of the engineer company died, and Captain Swift and twenty of the men were left in hospital at Matamoros, when the company finally left the latter place.

Before giving an account of our first march in the enemy's country, it may be well to state here that with two exceptions, the enlisted men of the engineer company were native born, and all but four of them were raw recruits. Each of these four had served, with credit, during one or more terms of enlistment in the regular army. Three of them were promptly made sergeants, and the fourth was a musician (bugler).

All of the recruits but one were very carefully selected material out of which to form, as soon as practicable, skilled engineer soldiers. The one exception was a short, fat, dumpy, Long Island Dutchman— a good cook especially enlisted by Captain Swift to cook for the men. He was given the pay and rank of artificer of engineers. The men looked upon him more as a servant of theirs than as a fellow soldier. He was well satisfied with his position, prided himself on his special duties, rather looked down upon "soldiers"—and was impudent by nature.

All went well enough with the "cook" until he was required to take his place in the ranks, at regular bi-monthly "muster, and inspection" for pay. His performance on that occasion was so grotesquely awkward that I directed he should be put through the "squad-drill" by one of the sergeants, who was a thoroughly competent, but rather severe, drill-master.

The "cook" felt that his rights were invaded, in requiring him to submit to be drilled. The sergeant made no progress in teaching him. After three days' trial, he reported to me that he was mortified, and ashamed, to have to admit he could do nothing with "that cook"; and he asked to be relieved from the duty of drilling him. In reply to my question: "Can't you make him obey you?" He replied: "No—the only thing I can do is to kill him"; and added: "When that kind of thing has to be done, in this company, my understanding is, the lieutenant in command is the only one who has the right to kill."

I relieved the sergeant, and told him I would take the "cook" in hand at the next drill. On the following day, I marched him off into the dense chaparral, on the bottom lands near Matamoros. After following obscure paths, about three miles in their windings through the jungle, I halted him in a small open space a few hundred yards from the company camp. He thought, no doubt, we were five miles from camp—in boundless wilderness—whilst, in fact, we were at no time five hundred yards away.

I told him of the report that had been made to me of his disobedience, informed him that I had brought him into the chaparral for the purpose of compelling him to obey me; called his attention to the fact that we were in the enemy's country in time of war; all of our lives were in peril, and that persistent disobedience on the part of any officer or soldier to the legal authority of those over him was punishable with death; that I did not propose to place him before a Court Martial but would kill him, if he did not implicitly obey an order I proposed then and there to give him.

I measured 15 paces in front of him and placed a small white chip on the ground, called him to "attention," ordered him to place his eyes on that chip, and told him if he removed them from it before I gave the command "rest," I would run him through with my rapier.

I then drilled him at the manual of arms for about 20 minutes. Large beads of perspiration rolled down his face—he began to totter on his feet—and I gave the command "rest." He had not taken his eyes from the chip.

At the command "rest," he drew a long sigh of relief and uttered a subdued but prolonged "Oh." I asked him if he now thought he could obey the sergeant. He replied: "yes, I will obey anybody."

I told him I would temporarily withdraw what I had said about killing him, and would put him on his good behavior. I drilled him about two hours longer; and then took him, by a circuitous route, through the jungle, back to camp. He was obedient enough thereafter.

When the war had ended and I was relieved from duty with the company, one of the men told me that "the cook," on his return from the drill I had given him said: "The Lieutenant took me way off, ever so far, in the chapparal, and told me he took me there to kill me if I didn't mind him. The little devil meant it, and would have done it too, if I had fooled with him like I had done with the sergeant."

Except this *case*, of "the cook," there had been no difficulty in bringing the men of the company to a high standard of drill and discipline as an infantry company, and a reasonable degree of proficiency in the school of the engineer soldier. But, on their first march into the enemy's country, they were called upon to do an immense amount of hard work not specially referred to in their preliminary instruction.

The March from Matamoros to Victoria and Tampico

By special orders from General Taylor, brought by Major George A. McCall[6] to Captain Swift, the latter was charged with the duty of repairing the road from Matamoros to Victoria, and making it practicable for artillery and the baggage train; and to do this, if possible, so that the whole command might make its prescribed daily marches and arrive at Victoria on a named day. Captain Swift was authorized to call upon the commander of the forces, on this march, for such assistance as might be needed to perform the work; and was directed to do no more to the road than was barely sufficient to enable the trains to pass over it. It was not expected that we would ever have occasion to pass through that region again; and it was not proposed to make a permanent road for the benefit of Mexicans.

Captain Swift being sick in hospital, the foregoing instructions were given to me, as Commander of the company, by Major McCall, who, in the capacity of Adjutant-General of the forces under General Patterson,[7] accompanied him on this march.

Under orders from General Taylor, the company of engineers, reduced to two officers and forty-five enlisted men for service, marched from Matamoros on the 21st of December, 1846, with a column of volunteers under General Patterson, to join General Taylor's army at Victoria. We arrived at the latter place on the 4th of January, 1847. A great deal of work had been done by details of volunteers and the engineer company in making the road practicable for artillery and baggage wagons. Without dwelling upon daily operations, the following statement of the manner in which we made our way across a difficult stream may be of interest.

About noon one day I was informed by Major McCall, who had ridden ahead of the working party, that there was an exceedingly difficult "river-crossing" about one mile in front, and that he feared we would be detained there for, perhaps, two days. I galloped forward to the place designated. It looked ugly. The banks of the stream were something more than 100 feet high and quite steep. Guiding my horse down to the water's edge, I crossed the river, which was from two to three feet deep, and about one hundred yards wide. The bottom was fair enough, until within a few yards of the opposite shore, where it was soft mud. Getting through this with some difficulty I rode to the top of the bank on the far side.

To make an ordinary practicable road across that stream would require two or three days' work of several hundred men. It seemed a clear case for the free use of drag ropes to let the wagons down into the stream on the near side, and haul them up the opposite bank.

It was plain to me that with a working party of two hundred men—which was the greatest number we could supply with tools—a straight steep ramp could be cut on both banks in six or eight hours' hard work. The greatest difficulty would be encountered in getting out of the stream on the far side.

Returning quickly to where I had left Major McCall, I asked him to give me a working party of about 800 men, told him I would find use for that number and that in my opinion, with that force, the wagon train could be put across the stream before dark. The commanding General thought my requisition for the working detail was extravagant, as we scarcely had tools enough for a quarter of that number of men. But the detail was ordered, as called for, to report to me. In the meantime the engineer company and its train was taken to the crossing, and the character of the work to be done there was explained to the men.

Leaving Lieutenant McClellan with a portion of the company to take charge of the near bank, directing him to halt there about

300 of the working party and send about 500 to me on the oppo-site bank, I crossed the stream with the rest of the company and explained to them the work to be done on that side, particularly the means to be used in getting out of the river. On each side of the stream the working party was divided into three "reliefs," or relays—with one hundred men or more held in reserve, to meet contingencies.

The working party arrived in good season, tools were promptly distributed to the first "relief" on each side of the river, and the men were told that, if they would work as at a "corn-shucking-match," or as if the "house was on fire," they would be let off in an hour, or less, depending on the rapidity and effectiveness of their work. It was to be a race against time. I wanted all the work there was in them, and wanted it inside of an hour.

Before the hour was up the "first relief" on each side of the river, was ordered to stop work, drop their tools, get out of the road and take to the bushes. The "second relief" was immediately marched into the vacated places, seized the tools, and worked like the first—and on the same conditions. So with the "third relief"; and, inside of three hours from the time the work began, the engineer wagons were crossing the river. They soon moved on, leaving the rest of the forces to follow at their leisure.

The volunteer officers afterwards complained to me that the "wild work" on the banks of that river had "scattered" their men so badly, it was several days before they could be again got into their proper places.

This case was an exception—a frolic. The usual daily work on the road was more regular and continuous, without disorder.

It may perhaps not be out of place here to mention, that about the time I sent the "first relief" into the bushes, and set the "second relief" to work under the directions of men of the engineer com-pany, the commander of the forces, with his staff, arrived on the bank where McClellan was in charge, and asked for me. He was told that I was on the opposite bank. Just at that time the confusion and wild yells of the "first relief" and the loud cheers of the "sec-ond relief" when told that they, too, would be let off inside of an hour, provided they would work as if engaged in a "corn-shucking match," astounded the general, and had to him the appearance of disorder, perhaps mutiny.

On asking Lieutenant McClellan what it meant, the latter replied: "It is all right; Lieutenant Smith has the larger portion of the engineer company with him on that bank; and I can see him, and men of the company near him in the road, all of whom seem to be quietly giving instructions to the new working party."

After starting the "second relief" to digging in the road, I had gone to the brow of the bank overlooking the work which was being done, mostly by my own men in the river, where the road was to leave it. The engineer sergeant in charge of that work informed me that he was then in immediate need of about twenty additional men. The reserve working force was not far from me. I called out for a sergeant and twenty men, without arms or accoutrements, to come to me. Pointing to the river, just under the place at which I was standing, I directed the sergeant of this reserve party to take his men down at once and report to the engineer sergeant in charge there. The bank was precipitous. The sergeant of the reserve working party said that he would take his men back about one hundred yards, and go down by the road on which the "second relief" was working. I demurred, and told him again to take his men straight to where they were needed. He still hesitated. I pushed him over the brow of the bank, and he went headlong into the river. I then ordered his men to follow him. They did it with a cheer and regular "Comanche-whoop"—sliding down the slope, which was too steep to stand on.

This scene, too, was witnessed from across the river by the General of the forces and his staff. I did not know they were there; but if I had, it would have made no difference; I was in charge of the working party, and in haste to finish that *special job*.

On our arrival at Victoria, the company was relieved from duty under General Patterson, and I was directed to report to the headquarters of General Taylor. On the 12th of January the company was ordered to report to General Twiggs.[8] With two companies of the line to furnish additional details for labor when required, I was charged with the duty of making the road between Victoria and Tampico practicable for wagons. These three companies left Victoria on the 13th.

The following extracts from my official report of the operations of the Engineer Company for the month of January, 1847, illustrate, in part, the difficulties met with.

"The first day, (out from Victoria) we had three bad boggy brooks to cross; besides a great deal of cutting to do with axes in order to open the road; and many bad ravines and gullies to render passable. To make a bridge, across a boggy stream, with no other material than the short, knotty, hard and crooked chaparral bush, was no easy matter. The first day's march was about ten miles—we encamped about sunset after a very hard day's work."

In order to shorten the route and save the forces one day's march, we were, for several days, working on a mule path "cut-off" from the main road.

"January 14th. The mule path was infamous. No wagon had ever traveled that road—the rancheros have a tradition of a bull-cart that, it is said, once passed that way. I believe, however, that the story is not credited. We worked from dawn of day until dark and encamped about six miles from where we started in the morning and about the same distance from the camp we wished to reach that day."

"January 15th. Another day's tremendous hard work."

"January 16th. We had again a very severe day's work."

"January 17th. Road improved very decidedly, but still a good deal to do. We managed, by getting a little ahead with our repairs after the army encamped for the night, to get along without seriously delaying the column."

We arrived at Tampico on the 23rd. The distance from Victoria to Tampico is 120 miles; [the] whole distance from Matamoros to Tampico, by way of Victoria, is 354 miles.

Although the service was arduous, the men came through it in good health, and were all the better soldiers for the practical schooling acquired in that 350 miles of road making. After this experience, ordinary marches and drills were to them very light matters.

Tampico to Vera Cruz

From Tampico we sailed for Lobos Island and Vera Cruz, on a small schooner, the Captain of which was a brave little Frenchman, who was not acquainted with the Mexican Gulf coast, and was not provided with accurate instruments for taking observations. Late one afternoon the clouds rolled away, and we distinctly saw the snow-clad peak of Orizaba. This was the first intimation to us that we were "somewhere" near Vera Cruz. In a very short time we saw opposite to us a large fleet of vessels at anchor.

We were south of Vera Cruz and were passing Anton Lizardo, the place to which we were bound. But a reef was between us and the anchorage where the fleet was quietly lying. The Captain of the schooner said he could cross the reef. Taking his place in the rigging from where he could better observe the breakers and the currents, the schooner tacked here and there, rapidly and repeatedly, under the orders of the little Frenchman; and we were soon clear of the reef and breakers. It was now nearly dark. In a few moments after reaching the anchorage ground, we glided up a gentle slope, without perceptible shock; and the bow of the vessel was almost entirely out of water.

In less than twenty minutes thereafter a boat from one of our men-of-war pulled alongside; and when the officer in charge learned who we were, he said he would report at once to the naval commander; and had no doubt that the company with its effects would have to be landed on an adjacent island, while the schooner was being lightened and hauled off into deep water.

He said the movements of the little schooner, through the heavy surf, across the dangerous reef, had been watched from the naval vessels with intense anxiety, and expectation that we would be wrecked and all hands lost. This feeling was changed to admiration when it was seen that the schooner was being very skillfully handled in the difficult channel; and all rejoiced when they saw the unknown little craft safely in smooth water; but were surprised, immediately after, to see her put on a course that would inevitably run her aground.

We found that Captain Swift, with the convalescents from Matamoros on another vessel, had arrived before us. In the meantime Lieutenant J. G. Foster,[9] of the Engineer Corps, had been assigned to duty with the Company. He was with Captain Swift. I at once reported to the latter, and he resumed command of the Company; but the men remained on separate vessels.

Captain Swift was still very sick; to all appearance more feeble than when we left him at Matamoros. All the men he brought with him were convalescent. In a few days after our arrival at Anton Lizardo, an order was issued by General Scott[10] for the transports to move up next morning, towards Vera Cruz, with a view to landing the army on the main shore, opposite the Island of Sacrificios, two or three miles south of the city. On the morning of the day we were to make the landing the whole company was transferred to another vessel; and all were again together.

Early in the previous night, McClellan, who had just been aboard the vessel on which Captain Swift arrived, informed me that the latter proposed to lead the company ashore. Worth's[11] division was to land first, and the engineer company was temporarily assigned to that division. McClellan added: "The Captain is now too feeble to walk across the cabin of his vessel without assistance—the effort to lead the company in this landing will be fatal to him, and I told him I thought he ought not to attempt it. But, he looks upon me as a boy,[12] and I have no influence with him in this matter. You ought to advise him against this thing. If he attempts it, it will certainly kill him."

I fully agreed with McClellan in reference to the physical condition of the Captain; and the probable, if not certain, result of an attempt on his part to lead the company in the landing. But for me to advise him not to go ashore with us, was to request him to give me the command of his company in this important enterprise. I told McClellan that I felt a delicacy about the matter which made me hesitate to advise the Captain to give me the command of the company. He replied: "Yes, but this case is beyond mere delicacy. The act of leading the company ashore will kill him; and I think you can persuade him not to undertake it. You ought to try. I am sure he will not misconstrue your motive."

Urged thus, I pulled over to the Captain's vessel, after dark, found him alone in the cabin, and quickly told him why I came. He listened patiently to all I had to say; thanked me cordially for the interest I took in his physical welfare; said he fully appreciated the kindness shown; understood the motive which actuated the advice given; and added:"My mind is made up; I will lead the company in this landing; and would do so even if I knew that the bare attempt would certainly cost me my life."

The next afternoon, the Captain, standing by the gangway, directed the embarkation of about 20 men in the smaller of the two surf boats in which the company was to land. Just as that boat was ready to pull away to make room for the larger boat, I said to him: "I suppose I am to go with this detachment of the Company; and if so I must get aboard now." He replied "No. I wish you to go in the larger boat with me." To which I said: "All right," and added: "McClellan goes with the detachment?" The Captain said, "Yes."

When the larger boat for the rest of the Company came alongside I relieved the Captain at the gangway and superintended the embarkation of the men in that boat. The Captain was lowered over the side of the vessel in a chair; and I, when all else was ready to pull off, scrambled down into the closely packed boat, and took my place in the bow. Each boat was rowed by sailors from the fleet under the direction of a naval officer.

We had reason for anxiety in regard to the resistance we might meet with from Mexican batteries that could easily have been sheltered behind the sand hills immediately overlooking the open beach on which the landing was to be made. A single cannon-shot striking one of the closely packed surf-boats would probably have sent it, and all on board, to the bottom. The anxiety of the soldiers was to get ashore before such a fate should befall them. They cared very little for anything that might happen after they were on land; but wished to escape the danger of having the boats sunk under them by Mexican batteries.

When we were within five or six hundred yards of the beach all were startled by the whistling of shells and cannon balls close about our heads. This fire was soon understood to come from our Naval gunboats, and aimed at small parties of Mexican lookouts on shore. No resistance was made to the landing of Worth's division.

When we were within two or three hundred yards of the beach, I made my way, over the heads of the men to the stern of the boat where the Captain was seated; and said to him I thought the time had come for him to get to the bow, if he still intended to lead the company in going ashore.

For a moment the most painful expression I ever saw depicted on a human countenance marked his face. He rallied, however, almost immediately, and said: "I must, at the last moment, relinquish my command"; and added "I turn the command over to you until the company is formed in line on the beach."

I made my way quickly back to the bow; ordered the right file of the company, two stalwart corporals—thorough soldiers—to go to the stern of the boat, take their places near the Captain, keep their eyes on me after they reached him, spring into the water when they saw me jump from the bow, seize the Captain, place him on their shoulders or heads, and bring him to me in the line on shore, without a wet thread on him.

I informed the corporals that I had been placed in full command by Captain Swift; warned them he would probably resist their bringing him ashore; but no matter what he said or did, they must obey my orders. They did it. The corporals were athletes—over six feet in height, young and active. In the Captain's then physical condition he was as helpless as an infant in their hands.

The water where they went overboard was nearly up to their necks; but when they brought the Captain to me he was as dry as whilst sitting in the boat. He had resisted them more violently than I anticipated. In vain they explained to him that they were instructed by me to take him ashore without his touching the water. He ordered them to put him down, used all his force to compel them to do so, repeated his orders in no measured terms, and continued to denounce the corporals after they had placed him on his feet by my side.

He was wild with rage. I at once relinquished to him the command of the company, and said: "Captain, the corporals are not in

Gustavus W. Smith. Western Reserve Historical Society, Cleveland, Ohio

fault. They simply obeyed my order whilst I was, by your authority, in command of the company. Blame me, if you will, but exonerate them."

He apologized to the corporals for kicking, striking, and otherwise abusing them, and thanked them for the service they had rendered him. The termination of this incident made an indelible impression on the men in favor of their Captain.

That night the company slept among the sand hills a few hundred yards from the shore, undisturbed, except by a flurry of firing which occurred about 10 P.M., between a Mexican detachment and the Light battalion of Worth's division. This firing continued for a few minutes, and then all was quiet for the rest of the night.

About sunrise next morning, the company moved several hundred yards, into its position on the sand hills, on the right of Worth's division in the line of investment, facing Vera Cruz which was about two miles distant.

The Captain showed wonderful increase of vitality after he reached the shore. He conducted the company to its assigned place in the line of investment without much apparent difficulty in walking through the sand.

But three hours exposure to the hot sun was more than he could bear; his strength was gone. He lost consciousness and was, by my order, carried to the beach on an improvised litter. The sergeant of the party was instructed to report to the naval officer in charge of the surf boats, and in my name, request that Captain Swift be taken as soon as practicable to the steamer which was the headquarters of General Scott. That request was promptly complied with; but the Captain's vitality was exhausted. He was sent to the United States on the first steamer that left Vera Cruz after the landing was effected, and died in New Orleans within twenty-four hours after his arrival at that place.

Thus, the army and the country lost the services of one of the best officers of the U.S. Corps of Military Engineers; and the engineer company lost their trained Captain.

2
Engaged in Operations against Vera Cruz

Within a short time after Captain Swift was taken to the beach, I received an order, from General Worth, directing me to withdraw the engineer company from the line of investment {siege} and report to General Patterson. The latter instructed me to locate and open a road through the chaparral to the old Malibran ruins. This was accomplished by the middle of the afternoon. General Pillow,[1] who was to occupy a position beyond Malibran, requested me to take charge of a working party of his troops and, with the engineer company, locate and open a road along his line to the bare sand hills on his left. In this work we were somewhat disturbed by the fire of Mexican detachments.

On the 11th, the work of locating and opening the road along the line of investment was continued, the working party being still a good deal annoyed by both infantry and artillery fire. At 1 P.M., I reported to General Patterson that the road was opened, through the chaparral, to the bare sand hills. He ordered me to report, with the engineer company, to General Worth; and the latter directed me to report to the General Headquarters.

On the same day I was ordered by Colonel Totten, Chief Engineer, to find and cut off the underground-aqueduct which conveyed water into Vera Cruz. That business was effectually accomplished by the engineer company on the 13th.[2]

From that time, until the commencement of work upon the batteries and trenches, the engineer company and its officers were engaged in reconnoitring the ground between the picket line of our army and the fortifications of the city. My reports were made each night to the Chief Engineer. The night of the 15th, he pointed out to me, on a map of the city and its fortifications, the general location in which it was desired to place the army gun battery, on the southern prolongation of the principal street of the city, and within about six hundred yards of its fortifications. He directed me, with the engineer company, to closely examine that ground. I was informed by him, at the same time, that Captain R. E. Lee,[3] of the engineer corps, had discovered a favorable position for a battery, of six heavy naval guns, on the point of a commanding sand ridge, about nine hundred yards from the western front of the city; but no final decision would be made in regard to the naval battery until the army battery could be definitely located. He said General Scott was getting impatient at the delay; and I was directed to find, as soon as possible, a position that would satisfy the conditions prescribed, by the Chief Engineer, for an army battery.

I explained those conditions to McClellan and to Foster; and informed them that I would assign one-third of the company to each of them as an escort—[taking] one-third myself—and we would all three start, at daylight next morning, in search of a location for the required battery. It was necessary that we should be extremely careful not to get to fighting each other in the dense chaparral.

We found a location that complied with the conditions. In reporting this fact to the Chief Engineer, I added: "The communication with the battery will be very difficult—will require a great deal of work—and will be dangerous." He ordered me to take the engineer company to the selected ground, next morning, and lay out the battery; and said he would direct Lieutenant G. T. Beauregard,[4] who had supervised the construction of the field fortifications at Tampico, to assist in the work.

George B. McClellan. Western Reserve Historical Society, Cleveland, Ohio

At 2 P.M. that day the battery and magazine had been traced out, all necessary profiles carefully adjusted; and, the whole completed, {the company was} ready to commence throwing up the works. We had not been discovered by the Mexicans—though we could plainly see their sentinels on the walls; and occasionally hear words of command. After allowing the company to rest for a couple of hours we started to return to camp.

In going forward we had the Mexicans before us; and by exercising great care, at certain places, could avoid being seen. When our backs were turned to Vera Cruz I felt confident that we would soon be discovered and fired upon. I had cautioned the men to be as careful as possible; but, in spite of their best efforts, we were seen, and a heavy fire of artillery was opened upon us. The order to move at double-quick was immediately given. The company was conducted about three hundred yards, to a cut in a low sand ridge that had been formed by a road crossing that ridge. All got safely into the cut. The Mexican artillery fire, aimed at us, was continued for about twenty minutes. We had then before us an open level plain for five hundred yards. Soon after the fire upon us had ceased, I ordered the men to scatter and run rapidly across the plain until they reached a designated place of shelter behind high sand hills. Beauregard and I brought up the rear in this movement. The Mexicans re-opened their guns upon us whilst we were crossing the plain and continued to fire for some time after we reached the shelter above referred to.

When I reported the result of that day's work to the Chief Engineer, I urged him to permit a further examination to be made, for a location of the army gun battery, before attempting to construct the one we had just laid out.

He consented, and we made further reconnaissance the next day. In the meantime the pickets of Worth's division had been considerably advanced. On returning from an examination at the extreme front that day I came across a detachment of the Fifth Infantry {Regiment} not far from the Cemetery. Whilst explaining the object of my search to a group of four or five young officers, a person whom I took to be a veteran sergeant, said to me that he knew a good position for a battery, only a few hundred yards from where we then were. I asked him to describe it to me.

From the description he gave I thought the ground referred to would be a favorable site; and asked him to tell me definitely how to reach it. He offered to guide me to the place. On getting to the position I found that the conformation of the ground constituted almost a natural parapet for a six gun battery—requiring but little work to complete it for use. It afforded immediate shelter for men and guns.

It was not on the prolongation of the main street of the city, and it was farther from the enemy's works than the site where a battery had already been laid out. But the communications with the proposed new location were shorter, and could easily be made much safer—in every way better than was possible in the former case. I thanked my guide for pointing out the position; and told him I thought it would be adopted by the Chief Engineer.

After our return to the group of young officers, my "guide" was soon called away; and, I then asked one of them the name of that "fine old Sergeant" who had pointed out such a good location for the battery. To my amazement he replied; "That was Major Scott, the commander of our regiment."

The Major was enveloped in an ordinary soldier's overcoat and wore an old, common slouched hat. I had mistaken the "famous Martin Scott" for a "fine old Sergeant" of the line.

On my return to camp I reported all the facts to the Chief Engineer. The position first selected and laid out, for the army gun battery, was abandoned; and the location pointed out by Major Martin Scott was adopted.

The work of throwing up batteries, digging trenches, and making covered communications with them, was commenced on the night of the 18th by large working parties detailed from the line. After that time, the officers of the engineer company, including myself, were placed on general engineer service—supervising the construction of the siege works. All the engineer officers then with the army, except the Chief, were in regular turn detailed for that duty; each having some of the men of the engineer company to assist him.

After the work upon the army gun battery, the mortar batteries and the trenches had been fairly commenced, I was transferred to the naval battery and took my regular turn, with Captain R. E. Lee, and Lieutenant Z. B. Tower,[5] in superintending its construction. I was in charge of that work the day it opened its guns upon the fortifications of the city, having relieved Captain Lee that morning. Seeing him still in the battery, about the time the firing commenced, I asked him if he intended to continue in control; adding, "If so, I report to you for instructions and orders." He replied: "No. I am not in charge. I have remained only to see my brother, Lieutenant Sydney Smith Lee of the Navy, who is with one of the heavy guns. My tour of service is over. You are in control; and, if I can be of any service to you whilst I remain here, please let me know."

There had previously been a difference of opinion between Captain Lee and Myself in regard to the dimensions that should be given to the embrasures {openings through which the guns fired}. The Chief Engineer decided in favor of Captain Lee, and the embrasures were changed and made to conform to his views. In a very short time after the firing began one of the embrasures became so badly choked that it could not be used until the *debris* could be removed. Hastily renewing the blindage of brush-wood that had been used to conceal the work from view of the enemy during the construction, the detail of engineer soldiers then on duty, in the battery, cleared the embrasure of the obstructions, removed the blindage, and the gun resumed its fire. Just after that incident, I asked Captain Lee what he now thought in regard to the proper dimensions for the embrasures. He replied:"They must be made greater when the battery is repaired to-night."

The naval detachment had only forty rounds of ammunition; which was expended in about three hours, and the firing had to cease until the arrival of the next naval detachment. The latter, when it came into the battery, had only forty rounds of ammunition and was to serve until relieved, the next afternoon by a third naval detachment.

Before the ammunition of the first detachment was expended the embrasures were all in a very bad condition—the battery was almost entirely unserviceable; and before the second detachment arrived I caused the embrasures to be filled up, until the battery could be repaired that night and put in good condition for reopening the next day.

The second naval detachment came into the battery about the middle of the afternoon. The naval captain in command, without consulting me, ordered the embrasures to be cleared at once, with the intention of immediately opening fire. Perceiving what was being done by the sailors in re-opening the embrasures, I ordered them to stop; and asked by whose authority they were acting. On being informed that their orders came from the commander of the detachment, I asked them to point him out to me. I immediately introduced myself to him, as the engineer officer in full charge of the construction of the battery, and told him {that} if the embrasures were cleared the battery would still be unfit for service—that it could not be repaired until that night, and would then be put in better condition than it was when it first opened. The army gun battery would be ready next morning; and its fire, combined with that of the naval battery,

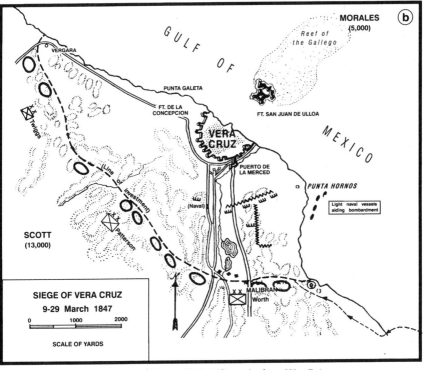

SIEGE OF VERA CRUZ
9-29 March 1847

SCALE OF YARDS

Department of History, U. S. Military Academy, West Point

after the latter was put in good condition, would be very effective. But, if the naval detachment opened fire that afternoon, the battery being unfit for service, its ammunition would be exhausted before night without hurting the enemy; and the battery would necessarily be silent the next day, when the army battery would open its fire.

The naval captain insisted that the embrasures should be cleared at once, and the firing resumed.

I protested against his clearing the embrasures and told him that, but for the appearance of the thing, I would leave the battery and take my men with me if he persisted in carrying out his intentions. I added: "I will remain here until regularly relieved, but will continue to *protest* against the course you propose to pursue."

He then told me that it was "the General's" order that he should open fire that afternoon as promptly as possible.

I asked him why he had not told me of that order in the first place; and added: "It is not customary for General Scott to give orders to engineer officers through officers of the navy. But, if you had told me in the beginning that he had ordered the battery to commence firing as soon as possible after you reached it, I would have accepted his order—coming to me through you."

To this he replied; "I did not say the order came from General Scott." I asked: "Whom did you mean when you said 'the General?'" He told me that he meant "General Patterson." To which I replied: "I receive no orders in reference to this battery except from General Scott or the Chief Engineer of the Army."

The naval captain finally said he would not open fire until next morning; provided I would report the circumstances to General Scott. I told him it was not usual for me to report my action direct to the General-in-Chief; but, I would report all the facts to the Chief Engineer as soon as I was relieved and had returned to camp, and he would report them to General Scott.

When I commenced to make my report to the Chief Engineer he stopped me; and said he was instructed to order me to report in person, to General Scott as soon as I reached camp.

I obeyed the order; and was very coldly and formally told by "The General": He had been informed it was my fault that the naval battery had not opened fire against Vera Cruz that afternoon. I answered: "I did prevent the fire being opened; but, that act was not a fault on my part; and I can convince you of the latter fact if you will give me a hearing."

He replied—still very coldly—"I hope you can do so." I then related to him, in full, all that had occurred—as briefly stated above—between the commander of the naval detachment and myself.

My reasons for opposing the opening of the fire of the battery seemed to produce little or no favorable impression on General Scott until I reached that part of the narrative in which I replied to the naval captain's statement that he meant General Patterson when he said *"the General."* I gave General Scott the exact words I had used in replying to the naval commander. At this he rose from his seat—came to where I was standing, and clasping one of my hands in both of his; said: "Thank God I have young officers with heads on their shoulders and who know how to use them." He added: "Your opinion, and your action, in this matter, would do credit to a Field Marshal of France"!

To which I made no reply, but thought to myself: "If there was a sergeant in the engineer company who, in view of the plain facts of this case, would not have known that the naval battery ought not to open fire that afternoon, I would reduce him to the ranks before night."

The following extracts from my official report of these operations may not be amiss in this connection:

"Whenever we have acted as a company I have been most ably and efficiently supported by Lieutenants McClellan and Foster; and I am proud to say that the non-commissioned officers and men of the company have shown great willingness and skill in the discharge of the important duties assigned them. Great part of our labors have {sic} been performed under fire. On such occasions I have had every reason to be satisfied with the cool deportment and conduct of the company.

"In conclusion I regret that I have to state, a serious blow was inflicted on the military pride of the engineer company in *not* allowing them to participate in the ceremonies of the surrender, when it was well understood that the troops having had most to do in the attack were selected to take a prominent part in the proceedings."

We all felt that, if our distinguished Captain had been with us, we would have been called on to take part in those ceremonies.

The Chief Engineer, Colonel Joseph G. Totten, in his report of operations against Vera Cruz,[6] says: "The obligation lies upon me also to speak of the highly meritorious deportment and valuable services of the Sappers and Miners, [engineer company] attached to the expedition. Strenuous as were their exertions, their number proved to be too few, in comparison with our need of such aid. Had their number been four-fold greater, there is no doubt the labors of the army would have been materially lessened and the result expedited." (Ex. Doc. No. 1. P. 245.)

3

After the Surrender of Vera Cruz
to the Occupation of Puebla

From the capitulation of Vera Cruz, on the 29th of March, until we left that place on the 13th of April, the engineer company was principally engaged in assisting engineer officers in making surveys of the fortifications and surrounding ground, in dismantling our own batteries, magazines, &c.; and aiding the Quartermaster's Department in landing and placing in depot the general engineer train {wagons} of the army.

In the meantime, on the 7th of April, I reported, through the senior engineer, to the Adjutant-General {in charge of administration} of the forces, that the engineer company would be ready to move with the advance division of the army on the 8th, if transportation {draft animals} for its train could be furnished. Transportation, together with orders to move with the advance division, were applied for. "The reply was that General Scott would, at the proper time, order such transportation for the engineer company as he deemed sufficient—and would, when it was his pleasure, order the company forward."[1]

Twiggs's division left on the 8th; Patterson's on the 9th; on the 11th Worth's division was ordered to move on the 13th; Quitman's[2] brigade had been previously sent on an expedition to Alvarado; the garrison of Vera Cruz was designated. Thus, every soldier in the army, except the engineer company, had received instructions either to go forward or to remain.

On the night of the 11th, in my evening report to the Adjutant of engineers I asked the Senior Engineer[3] then serving with the army when and where the engineer company was ordered; what I was ordered to do; and what transportation, if any, I was to have.

On these subjects not one word had been stated, in either written or printed orders, that had come to my knowledge. On the morning of the 12th, General Scott consented that the engineer company should, if possible, move with the General Headquarters, which left at 4 P.M. that day.

I then applied direct to the Chief Quartermaster for transportation. He told me that it was impossible to let me have any teams at that time—all the good teams had been taken by the army, General Worth was getting the last.

A positive order from headquarters was then procured by the Adjutant of engineers, requiring the Quartermaster's Department to furnish transportation for the engineer train, etc. The teams, such as they were, came into our camp about dark on the 12th. That night the wagons were loaded; and we started half an hour before daylight on the 13th.

The mules were wild, the teamsters could not speak English, some of them had never harnessed an animal; and it was soon apparent that the men of the company would have to put their muskets in the wagons and give their undivided attention to the mules. At 2 P.M., after struggling through the deep sand, west of the city, we struck the firm beach, and could make better progress, for about three miles, to Vergara, where the road leaves the coast, and again passes through deep sand.

In the meantime one team had become broken down and useless before we got beyond the city. In order to procure another I had to take some of my own men into the mule pen. Three Mexicans were given me to lasso the mules, and five men were required to put them in harness—seasick, wild, little animals. One teamster deserted; one had his hand, and another had his leg broken; and a number of mules in different teams were crippled.

At Vergara, half the load of each wagon was thrown out, before we entered upon steep ridges and deep sand immediately after leaving the beach. All the men were engaged in helping along the half loaded wagons. That night we slept in the sand ridges.

On the 14th, we reached Santa Fe, eight miles from Vera Cruz, threw out the half loads, and returned to Vergara. Before we again reached the beach, the men had actually to roll the empty wagons up every hill, the mules not being able to drag them. By 10 P.M., we were again at Santa Fe, having killed three mules {through overwork}, and the men being worked nearly to death. Fortunately for us, several good mules that had escaped from preceding army trains came out of the chaparral to our feed troughs, were caught, and "pressed" into engineer service.

From Santa Fe the road was much better, but at every hill the men had to take to the wheels and help the mules—this too, after throwing out half the load at the foot of some of the steeper hills. In this way, we reached the National Bridge, at 3 P.M. on the 16th.

General Worth's division was about starting from that place to make a night march to Plan del Rio. He informed me that our army would attack the enemy, at the Cerro Gordo Pass, on the afternoon of the 17th; and said he desired that the engineer company should accompany his division. I informed him that my men and animals were utterly exhausted and could not go any further without several hours {of} rest. But I assured him that we would be in Plan del Rio by noon of the next day. We rested at the National Bridge until 11:30 P.M., on the 16th, and reached Plan del Rio, about 11 P.M., on the 17th.

At Cerro Gordo

Soon after our arrival at Plan del Rio, I was ordered to detail an officer and ten men of the engineer company to report to General Pillow for temporary service with his division. Lieutenant McClellan was placed in charge of that detail.

With the remainder of the company, I was directed to report to Captain R. E. Lee, then acting as Chief Engineer of Twiggs's division; who instructed me to allow the men to rest, whilst I accompanied

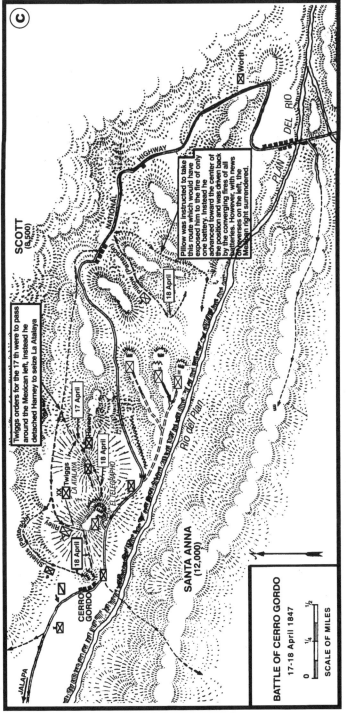

Twiggs orders for the 17 th were to pass around the Mexican left. Instead he detached Harney to seize La Atalaya

17 April

18 April

18 April

Twiggs
LA ATALAYA

Riley

EL TELEGRAFO

Harney

18 April

Shields Patterson

CERRO
GORDO

JALAPA

SANTA ANNA
(12,000)

Rio del Plan

18 April

SCOTT
(8,500)

NATIONAL HIGHWAY

Pillow was instructed to take this route which would have led him to the fire of only one battery. Instead he advanced toward the center of the position and was driven back by the converging fires of all batteries. However, with news of reverses on the left, the Mexican right surrendered.

Worth

PLAN DEL RIO

BATTLE OF CERRO GORDO
17-18 April 1847

0   ¼   ½

SCALE OF MILES

Department of History, U. S. Military Academy, West Point

him to the front, where Twiggs's division was about going into action. Captain Lee informed General Twiggs that the engineer company was at Plan del Rio, and had been ordered to serve with his division. I was directed by General Twiggs to return at once, and bring the company to the front as soon as possible.

The action of the 17th was over before the engineer company arrived. Captain Lee directed me, with a portion of my men and a large detailed {provided by other units} working party, to construct a battery that night, in a position he had selected on the heights we had gained that afternoon. This was a work of some difficulty, owing to the rocky nature of the ground and the small depth of earth—in some places none, and nowhere more than a few inches.

After 3 A.M. on the 18th I sent one of my men to the foot of the hill to awaken Lieutenant Foster, who was sleeping there with the company, and tell him he must relieve me for the rest of the night.

After putting Foster in charge I started to join the company—and became sound asleep whilst walking down the hill. Stumbling into a quarry hole, I found myself sprawling on a dead Mexican soldier— his glazed eyes wide open, within a few inches of mine. For a moment I felt that horror of a corpse which many persons have, at times, experienced. The probability that, in a short time after daylight—in storming the strong position of the enemy—I might be as dead as the man upon whom I was lying, forced itself upon me.

Before I could regain my feet streams of men were rushing past me in the darkness; and I heard and recognized, the voice of Lieutenant Peter V. Hagner,[4] of the Ordnance {artillery}, calling in no measured tone or language, upon these stampeded men to stop. Whilst promptly aiding Hagner to bring the fugitives to a halt, I forgot the dead Mexican, and the whole train of thought connected with the corpse.

When something like order was restored on the hillside I learned from Lieutenant Hagner, that he had been detailed to take one of our heavy guns up the hill to the battery. A regiment of Volunteers had been placed at his disposal to man the drag-ropes. Their arms had been left at the foot of the hill. On finding his way blocked by trees, Hagner had sent to procure axes from the engineer train; and in the meantime the regiment at the drag-ropes had been permitted to lie down. Of course they went to sleep. Suddenly awakened by a false alarm that the Mexicans were upon them, they rushed down the hill to get their arms. Hagner soon procured the required axes and the gun was delivered at the battery in good time.

At daylight I was again at the battery. A slight epaulment {embankment} had been finished for three pieces of artillery, the platforms were laid, and the guns in position. I was then instructed by Captain Lee to send ten men to report to him for special service; to order Lieutenant Foster with eight additional men, to report to him (Lee) for the purpose of opening a road for the light artillery around the foot of the heights; and I was ordered, with the rest of the company, to report to Colonel Harney, who was then in command of Persifor Smith's brigade,[5] of Twiggs's division.

I was instructed to accompany that brigade when it moved forward to attack the enemy in position on a hill immediately in front of, and higher than, that on which our battery had been constructed. The Mexicans were in strong force on the higher hill.

From our lower position we could not clearly see their lines nor determine how they were fortified. The hill they occupied was flat on top and their lines were set back from the crest of the precipitous slope which faced us. The storming brigade was ordered to halt and reform just before reaching the top of the higher hill. At this point they were below the plane of the enemy's fire, and were when lying down, perfectly protected. In this position they were ordered to rest, until the order should be given to rise, {and} charge the enemy's works by open assault.

When the line was thus formed, I requested Colonel Harney not to give the order to charge until I could go on the plateau, get a clear view of the enemy's works, and report their character. I soon informed him that their main line was not more than forty or fifty yards from where our men were then lying, that the fortifications were very incomplete, offered no effective obstacle, and we could dash over the works without a halt. I then ordered my men to drop their tools and use their muskets.

Whilst I was making this report to Colonel Harney, our attention was drawn to quite a sharp fire that the Mexicans had suddenly opened from a point close to the left flank and in the prolongation of our line. I told him I was certain there were no fortifications in that position; and I had seen no troops there. The fire increased from that direction, and Colonel Harney ordered me to proceed rapidly with my men to the left of our line, direct two companies on that flank to wheel at once, to the left; and when he gave the order to charge, these two companies and the engineers would move to the left against the force that was firing upon us from that side.

These dispositions on our left were made in a very few moments, and the order to charge was given immediately thereafter. The brigade sprang up, dashed over the short intervening space, and were almost instantly inside of the Mexican incomplete works.

After a short, but bloody, hand to hand struggle, in which bayonets, swords, pistols, and butts of muskets were freely used, the Mexicans retreated in great disorder. The troops that had been faced to the left just before the order to charge was given, immediately found themselves in the midst of a detachment of Mexicans, in a nest of surface quarry holes which gave them protection from distant fire and effectually concealed them from view until we were among them. The struggle here was hand to hand, and sharp for a short time. But they were driven from their quarry holes, back on their main line, which gave way, and their own guns {cannons} were turned upon them before they could get off the field.

Thus, Persifor Smith's brigade, under Colonel Harney, carried, and held possession of, the key-point of the battlefield of Cerro Gordo.

After the battle the various details of engineer soldiers joined in the pursuit of the enemy were collected together at Encerro, and the company remained with Twiggs's division until it reached Jalapa. At this place it was furnished by the Chief Quartermaster with the finest mule teams in the army. This gave great satisfaction to the men who had struggled so hard to get the engineer train forward, through deep sand, from Vera Cruz. To add to their elation, they had now left the "hot lands" of the coast behind them, had reached a temperate climate, 4,000 feet above the level of the sea, had escaped

Winfield Scott. Western Reserve Historical Society, Cleveland Ohio

the dread *vomito*[6] of Vera Cruz, and had participated closely in the great victory gained by Scott's army at Cerro Gordo.[7]

From Jalapa, Worth's division led the way, the engineer company at its head. During the halt of a few days, at Perote, I procured the transfer of First Sergeant David H. Hastings, from the Third

Artillery to the engineer company. He was considered one of the best sergeants in the army, and was at once made first sergeant of the engineer company. Previous to that time we had only an acting first sergeant. The company entered Puebla with Worth's division, and on the arrival of General Scott at that place we were again ordered to report to general headquarters.

During the three months delay of the army, at Puebla, awaiting reinforcements before moving into the valley of Mexico, the regular instruction of the company—both as infantry and as engineer soldiers—was resumed. Besides the "School of the Sapper" as taught them before they left the United States, the men were now instructed, theoretically and practically, in the "School of the Miner." They were engaged too in work upon the fortifications of Puebla; and had practice in loop-holing walls {cutting holes through which small arms could fire}, and received instruction for placing towns, villages, etc. in a state of defense. Whilst at Puebla the company received the sad news of the death of their Captain.

General Scott, in his official report of the battle of Cerro Gordo, says; "Lieutenant G. W. Smith led the engineer company as part of the storming force [under Colonel Harney], and is noticed with distinction." (Ex. Doc. No. 1, p. 263.)

General Twiggs, in his official report of the same battle, states: "Lieutenant G. W. Smith, of the engineers, with his company of Sappers and Miners, joined Colonel Harney's command in the assault on the enemy's main work, and killed two men with his own hand." (Ex. Doc. No. 1, p. 278.)

In Colonel Harney's official report of this battle it is stated:"Lieutenant G. W. Smith, of the engineers, with his company, rendered very efficient service in his own department, as well as in the storming of the fort." (Ex. Doc. No. 1, p. 281).

4

From Puebla to Churubusco

On the 7th of August, 1847, the advance of General Scott's army, Twiggs's division, the engineer company leading, left Puebla and commenced the forward movement into the valley of Mexico.[1] The company served with that division, until Worth's division was placed in the lead during the turning movement made by the army around Lake Chalco. In that movement the engineer company was at the head of Worth's division.

The road ran between the western border of the lake and a high range of hills which, in some places, rose from the water's edge. The road was narrow and rough and had been obstructed by rolling immense masses of stone upon it from the almost overhanging cliffs. These obstructions were of considerable height; they completely blocked our way; and at several points ditches had been cut across the road.

General Worth directed the Light Battalion, under Colonel C. F. Smith,[2] to advance and drive off the Mexicans who were firing upon us—ordered me to make the road passable for artillery and wagons as soon as possible—and notified me that the leading brigade would assist in that work when called upon. I immediately asked for a detail of 500 men; put them to work, at once, under the direction of the officers and men of the engineer company, and everything was progressing rapidly, when, to my surprise, Lieutenant J. C. Pemberton,[3] aide to General Worth, came up to me and insisted that the whole character of the operations should be changed. Whilst he was elaborating his views I cut him short by asking if he had any orders for me from General Worth. In the meanwhile the latter had reached the front, without either Pemberton or I being aware of his presence. Before the aide had time to reply to my question, General Worth, in a very peremptory tone called out "Come away from there Mr. Pemberton, and let Mr. Smith alone. This is his business—not yours."

In a few hours, the road was put in such condition that, by the use of drag-ropes and men at the wheels, we were enabled to pass artillery and wagons over the obstructions; and the column moved on without further material delay.

After reaching San Augustine, and passing beyond, the forward movement, now on the main road, or causeway, leading from Acapulco to the City of Mexico, was checked by fortifications about six hundred yards in our front. These fortifications crossed the road at San Antonio, and were occupied by the enemy in large force. The afternoon of the 18th of August was spent in reconnoitring that position.

About 3 A.M., on the 19th, I received an order to return to San Augustine with the engineer company and its train. In making our way from the head of Worth's division, along the main road, towards the rear, it was somewhat difficult to arouse the men of that division, who were sleeping on the road, and get them to clear the way for the passage of our wagons.

No explanation of the order for our return had been given. Just after the dawn of day, and before we were clear of the division, two soldiers on the side of the road were lighting a fire for the purpose of preparing coffee. As we passed them, one said to the other: "We are going not to fight to-day: Twiggs's division is going to fight." The other of the two replied, sneeringly: "What do you know about it?" To which the first answered: "Don't you see those young engineer officers, with the engineer company and their wagons? They are going back, to be sent on another road with Twiggs's division, we are not going to fight to-day." As we passed out of hearing of the two soldiers I said to McClellan, who was riding by my side: "Did you hear that?" He answered, "Yes and I consider it the handsomest compliment that could be paid to the engineer company. The private soldiers of this army understand that we are sent where the hardest work and hardest fighting are to be done— and always at the head of the leading division."

We reached San Augustine a little after sunrise, August 19. I will now quote directly from my official report of these operations.

"Orders were [at once] received, from the headquarters of the army, directing me to report to Captain R. E. Lee, of the Corps of Engineers, with the company under my command, and [I] was ordered by Captain Lee to take ten of my men, and select certain tools from the general engineer train, in addition to those carried along with the company. I turned over the command of the engineer company to Lieutenant McClellan, who, under the direction of Captain Lee, proceeded at once to commence the work on the road from San Augustine to Contreras.

"In about one hour and a half, I rejoined the command with the necessary implements for [a large working force in] opening the road. Captain Lee directed me to retain the men I then had with me, and to take charge of a certain section of the road, to bring forward my wagons as rapidly as possible, and to see that the road was practicable before I passed any portion of it. At this time my company was divided into five sections, each under an engineer officer directing operations on [different portions of] the road."

At Contreras

General Scott, in his official report, says, "By three o'clock, this afternoon [August 19th.], the advanced divisions came to a point where the new road could only be continued under the direct fire of 22 pieces of the enemy's artillery [most of them of large caliber] placed in a strong entrenched camp to oppose our operations, and surrounded by every advantage of ground, besides immense bodies of cavalry and infantry."

In my official report it is stated that "The head of the column having halted, I reached the front in time to receive instructions from Captain Lee to halt the company, collect the scattered parties, and to examine the road inclining to the left, while he went to the right. Lieutenants McClellan and Foster had been for some hours detached. Having gone about four hundred yards, I heard just ahead sharp firing of musketry; and immediately after met Captain McClellan, of the topographical engineers, and Lieutenant McClellan, of the engineer company, returning on horseback—they had come suddenly on a strong picket, and were fired upon. Lieutenant McClellan had his horse shot under him. Information of the enemy's picket being in our vicinity was reported to General Twiggs, who ordered a regiment of rifles forward. There being several engineer officers present when the rifles came to the front, I returned to my company, which had been for a short time left without an officer. Captain Lee about this time, sent back for Captain Magruder's battery, which was conducted by Lieutenant Foster, and placed in position by Lieutenant McClellan.

"The Third Infantry was ordered to support the battery. I moved forward with this regiment, taking my company and pack mules, loaded with tools, and placed my command under such shelter as could be found on the left, near the position occupied by the Third Infantry, and in rear of the battery. Meeting with Lieutenant McClellan, I directed him still to remain with the battery, but to order Lieutenant Foster to rejoin the company. In a few moments this officer reported to me, and brought information that the troops were preparing to storm the enemy's position.

"Riley's brigade had moved in advance by our right. Leaving the mules and tools, I moved the company forward, falling in with the brigade of General [Persifor] Smith. Captain Lee being present, with his consent I requested the General to allow the engineer company to fight in his brigade. He told me to take the head of the column, and to direct myself towards a church in a village, on the left of the enemy's battery—between it and the city. Whilst passing down the hill and crossing the ravine, the enemy were rapidly appearing [reinforcements from the direction of the city] on an eminence beyond the church. General Smith directed me to take my company as an escort, reconnoitre the village, and find out whether Colonel Riley's brigade was in the vicinity. I continued some distance beyond the church; and returned without seeing the brigade under Colonel Riley, which had, as I understood afterwards, advanced very near [the rear of] the enemy's battery. The reinforcements of the enemy upon the hill in our front were rapidly increasing. They had at this time probably ten thousand men, on the height, formed in line of battle. Towards dark Colonel Riley's brigade returned and joined the troops under the command of General Smith: too late, however, to allow time for forming the troops to attack the enemy [on the hill] in our front. Lieutenant McClellan joined me about this time in our movement on the village. Lieutenant Foster, who was on horseback, became detached with a few of the men, and did not rejoin me until after the action on the morning of the 20th.

"General Smith, very soon after dark, informed me that the enemy's main battery would be stormed, [in rear], at daylight on the morning of the 20th. This would open the road for artillery, and our communications with [the main army under] General Scott would be reestablished. I received orders to hold the engineer company ready to move at 3 A.M. and to take my place on the right of the rifles. On the morning of the 20th there was considerable delay in the movement of the brigade [raw troops] under General Cadwallader, by which General Smith's brigade, now under the command of Major Dimmick, First Artillery, was detained very nearly an hour. Part of the Eleventh Regiment [Cadwallader's brigade] lost its way, caused the Voltigeurs {skirmishers, called by the French term} to halt, thus throwing the brigade under Major Dimmick still further from Riley's, which had moved very soon after 3 o'clock. At the request of General Cadwallader, Major Dimmick ordered me to turn over the command of my company to the officer next in rank, and to move forward and conduct the troops that had lost their way. The whole force was by sunrise, or little after, halted in a sheltered position in rear of the enemy's battery." (Ex. Doc. No. 1, Appendix p. 67.)

I reported the cause of the delay to General Smith and requested instructions to rejoin my company; but he said he desired that I should remain with him for awhile. By his order, the three brigades were soon put in motion. I again asked him to permit me to rejoin my proper command. He replied "Not yet" and added: "I will soon give you instructions."

Because of a dense fog the delay in reaching the position in rear of the Mexican works was no material disadvantage. The fog began to disappear about the time I reported to General Smith. He was then on a ridge at a point about 600 yards in rear of the Mexican works. The three brigades were passing around the extremity of that ridge, several hundred yards in rear of the General. All was quiet in the lines of the enemy. There was another ridge south of the one on which General Smith was standing, and separated from it by a deep and very narrow valley. The sides of both ridges were precipitous; their tops sloped gently to the enemy's line.

General Smith informed me that Riley's brigade would pass partly beyond the extremity of the second ridge; then face to the left, and attack a strong Mexican detachment which was in position on that ridge, several hundred yards in rear of their works. Riley was ordered to drive that detachment and pursue it closely into the Mexican main lines. Cadwallader's brigade would go on when Riley faced to the left; and, as soon as he passed Riley, Cadwallader would also face to the left and come into action on Riley's right. Smith's own brigade would turn to the left before reaching the extremity of the second ridge. The Third Infantry and First Artillery would advance in the deep valley between the two ridges; whilst the Rifle Regiment, with the engineer company leading, would ascend the steep slope of the second ridge, and get into position on the flank, or rear, of the Mexican detachment which Riley was to attack in front. In the meantime the head of Smith's brigade had come within view, near the foot of the steep slope of the second ridge, and was moving towards the Mexican main line.

General Smith pointed out to me the route to be taken to reach the top of the second ridge; and ordered that the engineer company and rifles should bear to the right, and on getting near the Mexican detachment, remain concealed, and quiet, until Riley's brigade became well engaged; then join in the attack and pursuit of that detachment.

With these specific instructions, I was ordered to rejoin my company; and Lieutenant Beauregard was directed to take general charge of the movements of Smith's brigade. When Beauregard and I reached the top of the second ridge we found we were 50 yards, or less, in rear of the Mexican detachment, which was facing Riley. All was quiet. In a very few moments Riley's fire commenced.

The engineer company, followed by the rifle regiment, was then forming in line, under cover, in rear of the Mexican detachment, whose attention was concentrated on Riley, in their front. We were between that detachment and the Mexican works. A small portion only of the Rifle Regiment was in line, when the firing with Riley became very severe, and the order was given for the engineer company and rifles {riflemen} to rise and fire into the backs of the enemy. That fire was very destructive. The Mexicans were astounded; {they} faced squarely about, and in a moment precipitately retreated.[4]

In my official report it is stated that: "Colonel Riley's advance became engaged with a very strong picket, some 300 yards or more from the rear of the [enemy's] battery, near the crest of the ridge; the engineers and rifles came up at once in position to take the picket in rear, delivered a deadly volley within 50 yards, cheered and rushed on. The enemy's force fled; the head of our column crossed the line of their retreat, which brought the right of the column [engineer company and rifles] conducted by Lieutenant Beauregard, in contact with the Seventh Infantry, which formed the left of Colonel Riley's brigade. I went into the enemy's battery with the colors of the Seventh Infantry, my company immediately behind me. The enemy, or at least a portion of them, stood to their guns well, and delivered a fire of grape into our troops when the head of the column was within 25 yards of their pieces. Our troops followed the retreating enemy without halting until they were beyond the reach of our musketry. Lieutenant Beauregard then strongly advised that the troops be halted and formed. A short time afterwards General Twiggs, came up. The pursuit was resumed. At San Angel we had an unimportant skirmish." (Ex. Doc. No. 1, Appendix, p. 68.)

The following additional quotations from my official report are not deemed irrelevant:

"In the action of the morning of the 20th—the battle of Contreras—my men acted with great gallantry; their promptness in obeying every order, and the effect with which they used their muskets, entitle them all to the highest praise. In my report to the chief engineer in the field, I shall make special mention of all who, to my knowledge, particularly distinguished themselves. I will mention here, First Sergeant D. H. Hastings, of the engineer company, who, by his gallant conduct and soldiery bearing, in this action, richly deserves promotion to the rank of commissioned officer in the army. Sergeant Hastings was slightly wounded by my side in the battery. Sergeant [S. H.] Starr attracted my particular attention by his gallant and efficient conduct. Sergeant Starr was the ranking non-commissioned officer with the detachment of the engineer company which accompanied Colonel Harney's command at the battle of Cerro Gordo. I would recommend him for promotion [to the grade of commissioned officer in the army].

"Artificer W. H. Bartlett attracted my particular attention by [his] cool and steady gallantry; Artificer A. S. Read shot the color bearer of the Twelfth Regiment of artillery, and secured the color.

"Lieutenant Foster was at this time, as I have before remarked, detached with a portion of the company; and, at the head of his men, led the Ninth and Twelfth Regiments of Infantry in their attack on the flank of the retreating column at Contreras.

"Lieutenant McClellan, frequently detached, and several times in command of the engineer company, is entitled to the highest praise for his cool and daring gallantry, on all occasions, in the actions of both the 19th and 20th." (Ex. Doc. No. 1, Appendix, p. 69.)

In the pursuit, we passed through the village of San Angel; and near that place, were again halted. During that halt, I noticed a large, high building, in an extensive open field, five or six hundred yards to the North. I was satisfied that from the top of that building, with a powerful field glass which was a portion of the engineer company equipment, I would be able to get a good view of the level country for miles around, and obtain quite definite knowledge of the positions and movements of the main Mexican forces.

I communicated my wishes to Major Loring; and asked him if he felt authorized to support the engineer company, with the Rifle

Regiment, in a close reconnaissance of the building I pointed out. He laughingly replied: "I have been directed by General Smith to follow you and your company—of course I will go with you."

We had not proceeded more than two hundred yards towards the building when we were overtaken by Lieutenant Van Dorn,[5] Aide to General Smith, who brought an order requiring the Rifle Regiment and the engineer company to return to the head of the column on the road. I told Van Dorn the purpose I had in view, asked him to explain the matter to General Smith, and expressed my conviction that he would approve the movement, when he knew its object. Van Dorn replied: "General Smith was very peremptory. I am directed to see that you and Major Loring, with your respective commands, return at once." On our way back, Van Dorn said that General Pillow had reached the front and taken control; and his belief was that General Pillow had ordered General Smith to recall the engineer company and the Rifle Regiment. A short time thereafter we moved from San Angel to Coyocan, where the head of the column again halted; and [the column] was soon joined by General Scott.

There is good reason to believe that observations, which could easily have been made from the roof of the high building above referred to, would have resulted in obtaining such information in regard to the Mexican position at the Convent of Churubusco and at the *tete-de-pont* {bridgehead}, as would have enabled General Scott to complete the rout of the Mexican Army without incurring the additional loss of nearly one thousand men in killed and wounded.

At Churubusco

The following quotations are taken from my official report:

"Between 12 and 1 o'clock, P.M., [August 20, 1847] I received orders to move, from the village of [Coyocan] immediately after the rifle regiment, on a road intersecting the road from San Antonio to Mexico, in order to cut off the enemy already retreating from San Antonio.

"I had not gone two hundred yards when I received orders to countermarch and move on another route intersecting the road from San Antonio to the city nearer to Mexico. [The latter road led nearly due east, parallel to the front of the earthworks at the Convent, distant from those works about 250 yards]. The regiment of riflemen continued on the road on which I first started. [This road led south-east from Coyocan]. The company took its place [again] at the head of the column [Twiggs's division]. The column was halted by General Twiggs, and I was directed by him to send an officer in advance to see the position of a battery reported to be not far in front. Lieutenant McClellan was sent on one road; and Lieutenant Stevens of the engineers, was directed by General Twiggs, to take another. Both officers soon returned and reported a battery in front of a convent, the roof and steeples of which were in plain view of the head of the column and within 700 yards. The roof was crowded with troops; the battery was masked by intervening trees and cornfields. General Twiggs then directed these officers to make a closer reconnaissance and ordered my company as an escort. Having proceeded 500 yards, we saw [Mexican] troops on our right, left, and in front. A lancer {light cavalryman} was taken prisoner. Lieutenant Stevens directed me to take the prisoner to the general and request an additional escort of two companies. We were at this time about 300 yards from the battery, but it was still almost masked from view. I delivered the prisoner and the message to General Twiggs, and returned at once to my company which I had left in charge of Lieutenant Foster. Lieutenant Stevens joined General Twiggs whilst I was with him. When I resumed command of the company, Lieutenant McClellan reported to me that *our troops were already engaged in our front*; having, apparently, turned the battery and convent by our right. One of General Twiggs's staff [Lieutenant W. T. H. Brooks, A. A. {Acting Assistant} Adjutant General, Twiggs's division], was present and informed us that the rifles with Captain Lee of the engineers, were reconnoitring the same works, and had gone to our right considerably farther from the battery than we then were. We all concurred in opinion that the rifles were engaged with a vastly superior force. There was at this time no firing of artillery. I ordered Lieutenant McClellan to report the result of his observations to General Twiggs. He did so, and on the recommendation of Lieutenants Stevens and McClellan, in which I concurred, the First Regiment of Artillery was ordered to support the rifles. The firing on the right increased; it was evident that several thousands of the enemy were pouring a heavy musketry fire into our troops on the right. The tops of the convent and the surrounding walls were lined with troops; the roof was literally covered. Lieutenant Stevens was of opinion that a few rounds of grape would disperse these masses and relieve our troops already engaged [on the right] from a destructive plunging fire. He went back to the general, leaving myself the senior engineer then in front of the [convent] battery. The fire had now become very brisk upon my [reconnoitring] party; having placed the company under the best shelter at hand, with Lieutenant Foster I proceeded to examine the works to determine the number, character and position of the pieces of artillery. Nothing heavier than a 4 or 6-pounder had yet been fired." (Ex. Doc. No. 1, Appendix, p. 69.)

In my official report it is further stated that: "The troops had become engaged in our front within ten minutes after a reconnaissance had been ordered by General Twiggs, and before the officer whom I was escorting had been able to make a single observation."

In my official copy of that report, I find the following sentence, which is not in the printed report:

"Deeply do I regret that the attack, in advance of the reconnoitring party, precipitated the attack on our side, and involved us in action against we knew not what."

The force which became engaged, far to our right—before the reconnaissance, supported by the engineer company, fairly commenced, was the advance of Worth's division pursuing the Mexicans who had abandoned their strong works at San Antonio.

Captain James L. Mason, engineer of Worth's division, says, in his official report, that the works attacked by that division, and "so gallantly stormed, had not been reconnoitred."

The engineers in front of the convent, being informed that the rifles with Captain Lee had gone to our right considerably farther from the battery, advised that the rifles be supported by an additional regiment. The same engineers advised that one gun [cannon] be sent to the front to drive the Mexicans from the roof of the convent, and thus relieve our troops on the right from a destructive plunging fire.

The additional escort of two companies, asked for by the reconnoitring engineers, had not come to the front. After Lieutenant Stevens had gone back to General Twiggs, to have one gun with a few rounds of proper ammunition sent forward for the purpose of clearing the roof of the convent, the firing in our front, on the San Antonio road, had materially increased; and the fire from the convent, upon the engineer company, was becoming troublesome. There had been, to me, unexpected delay in bringing the one gun forward; and I determined, as already stated, to place the men under the best shelter at hand, and endeavor to make, in person, a closer examination of the works.

Resuming quotations from my official report—it is therein stated: "At this time the First Artillery came up to where I was. The lamented and gallant Burke, at the head of the leading company, asked which direction they were to take. I inquired what were his orders. He said that the regiment was ordered to support the rifles. I pointed to the smoke, which was all we could see by which to determine the position of our troops engaged in a cornfield on our right; told him that they reached their present place by moving farther to the rear, out of range of the works; and remarked to him that the fire through which he would have to pass in the direction he was going was very severe. He replied that they were ordered to move by that road to support the rifles. The First Artillery filed by and soon encountered, at a distance of 150 yards from the enemy, the heaviest fire of artillery and musketry, followed almost immediately after [by that] brought to bear upon Taylor's battery, which had been ordered to fire upon the convent; and, in selecting a place suitable for managing the guns, had most unfortunately been placed, entirely exposed, directly in front of a well constructed battery with heavy pieces firing in embrasure.

"As the First Artillery filed by me, I ordered my company to be formed, determined to go on with the reconnaissance; and if possible, send back to the general [Twiggs] accurate information in reference to the works of the enemy and the position of our own troops, which at that time I could not understand. In moving forward, I was opposite the centre of the [First] Artillery which inclined more to the left, toward the battery, whilst I kept nearer the [principal road leading almost due east from Coyocan]. The ground was level, but some shelter was afforded to small bodies of men, by the ditches, maguey plant, etc. I ordered my men to separate, to shelter themselves as much as possible, [and] to keep within supporting distance of me. I proceeded about two hundred yards. I ordered every man to shelter himself in a small ditch which was fortunately near us; immediately after I heard the fire of Taylor's battery passing directly over my head. [When that fire commenced we were] in the corn-field, about half-way between Taylor's battery and the enemy. Requiring my command to lie close, with Lieutenant Foster, I made my way to an old ruined wall in the open space east of the corn-field, and from that position sent Lieutenant Foster to General Twiggs to report the extent of the line engaged on the right, that we were directly in front of the works [which were now in plain view], and that, in my opinion, the whole force under General Twiggs's command should turn the enemy's position by our left. Another battery [of the enemy] was seen distinctly to our right and far in rear of the Churubusco battery, apparently enfilading our line engaged on the right. General Twiggs had already sent Colonel Riley's brigade to turn the position by our left, and take the battery by the gorge. When Lieutenant Foster returned, I withdrew the company to a position of more safety, and joined General Smith and Lieutenant Stevens, who were near the place from which I started with the First Artillery. I remained there [under General Smith's order] until after the action." (Ex. Doc. No. 1, Appendix, pp. 70–71.)

That point was about 300 yards south-west of the convent. There were several adobe houses near, and from it a road along which there were some huts, led to the convent, and another road, almost due east, passed in front of the convent. In moving forward I had kept nearer the latter road, the First Artillery nearer the former. The point I reached in the open, east of the corn-field, was within less than 100 yards of the works at the convent, and there was every indication that these works did not extend along the western side of that building.

The place at which I joined General Smith and Lieutenant Stevens, after I returned from beyond the corn-field, was that at which it had been proposed to place one gun, under cover of the adobe hut; run it out by hand; fire, and run it under shelter again to reload. By this means, a few rounds of grape, canister, and shrapnel, could have cleared the roof of the convent.

In more senses than one, the firing of Taylor's battery through the ranks of the engineer company, in the corn-field, was a surprise to me. I learned from Lieutenant Stevens that, when he applied for one gun to be sent to the front, those in authority had deemed it best to send forward a whole battery, and place it in an open field, square in front of the fortifications.

The battle of Churubusco[6] was commenced, and mostly fought, haphazard, against the front of the Mexican fortified lines, without giving time for proper reconnaissance.

General Scott, in his official report of the battle, says: "Lieutenant Stevens of the engineers, supported by Lieutenant G. W. Smith's company of sappers and miners, of the same corps, was sent to reconnoitre the strongly fortified church or convent of San Pablo in the hamlet of Churubusco—one mile off [from Coyocan]. Twiggs with one of his brigades [Smith's, less the rifles] and Captain Taylor's field battery, were ordered to follow and to attack the convent. Major Smith, senior engineer, was despatched to concert with Twiggs the mode of attack, and Twiggs's other brigade [Riley's] I soon ordered to support him." (Ex. Doc. No. 1, p. 309.)

Major John L. Smith, senior engineer, says: "Lieutenant Stevens in the reconnaissance of the position of Churubusco, was assisted by Lieutenant McClellan and escorted by the company of sappers and miners. This company also participated in the operations of the right [of Twiggs's division]." (Ex. Doc. No. 1, p. 353.)

Major Dimmick, commanding the First Regiment of Artillery, says: "About 12 o'clock, P.M., the battalion was ordered to attack the position of the enemy at the church, reported by the engineers at the time to have but one piece of artillery. The point of attack selected by the senior engineer officer was masked by a corn-field, in front of which I deployed the battalion and ordered it to advance, when almost instantly a shower of musketry, grape and round shot poured upon us, under which the battalion advanced.

"The right had advanced to within one hundred yards of a regular bastion front, the curtain of which had four pieces in embrasure, besides nearly a thousand infantry, both of which kept up such a constant stream of fire that I could not advance further in line; I therefore ordered the men to cover themselves as well as possible. The left of the battalion advanced to within seventy yards of the work, being exposed to the fire of two pieces of artillery, *en barbette*, in addition to the fire of a considerable force of infantry, and some of them still nearer, so that they had a destructive fire on the cannoniers and infantry; which position the battalion maintained until the enemy were driven from their guns and bastion, when they were followed into their work and surrendered." (Ex. Doc. No. 1, Appendix, p. 78.)

Captain Francis Taylor, commanding light battery, says:"On reaching Churubusco, we came in sight of a church, where the enemy was posted, having, as was supposed, an entrenched battery thrown across the road. Troops were soon thrown forward to attack this place; and, after a short time, I was ordered to place the battery in a position where it was thought I could drive the enemy from the roof and walls of the church, and sustain the other troops in their efforts to carry this place by storm. On taking the position assigned me, I found we were exposed to a most terrible fire of artillery and musketry, of a regular entrenchment, covering the front of the church to which we were opposite, and which the intervening Indian corn hid from our sight at the time. Here I opened my battery, and it was served with great precision for about an hour and a half, notwithstanding it was exposed, during that time, to a constant shower of grape, round shot, shell and musketry. At last, finding my loss was becoming very great, and having succeeded in driving the enemy from the roof and walls of the church, and given to our troops such support as was in my power, I determined to withdraw the pieces." (Ex. Doc. No. 1, Appendix, p. 73.)

The connection between the reconnaissance of the engineers, and the operations of the First Artillery and Taylor's battery at

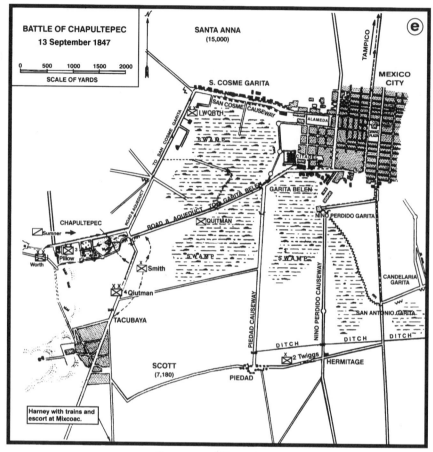

Department of History, USMA

Churubusco, has already been described in extracts taken from my official report.

In his official report, General Persifor F. Smith says: "Lieutenant G. W. Smith, in command of the engineer company, and Lieutenant McClellan, his subaltern, distinguished themselves throughout the whole of the three actions [19th and 20th at Contreras; and at Churubusco]. Nothing seemed to them too bold to be undertaken, or too difficult to be executed; and their services as engineers were as valuable as those they rendered in battle at the head of their gallant men. Lieutenant Foster, being detached from his company during the action at Contreras, did not fall under my notice; but in the action on the 19th and at Churubusco, he was equally conspicuous for his gallantry." (Ex. Doc. No. 1, p. 332.)

General Twiggs, in his official report, says: "To Lieutenant G. W. Smith, of the engineers, who commanded the company of sappers and miners, I am under obligations for his services on this and on other occasions. Whenever his legitimate duties with the pick and spade were performed, he always solicited permission to join in the advance of the storming party with his muskets, in which position his gallantry, and that of his officers and men, was conspicuously displayed at Contreras as well as Cerro Gordo." (Ex. Doc. No. 1, p. 325.)

5

Capture of the City of Mexico

During the armistice,[1] which was entered into just after the battle of Churubusco, and terminated on the 6th of September, the engineer company was quartered in the village of San Angel. On the 7th of September I received orders to move the company, its train, and the general engineer train of the army to Tacubaya.

Molino del Rey. That night I was ordered to detail an officer and ten men of the engineer company to report to General Worth. Lieutenant Foster was placed in charge of this detail. He and his men were on the right of the storming party of five hundred picked men, of Worth's division, which led the attack against Molino del Rey[2] on the morning of the 8th. In that attack Lieutenant Foster was very severely wounded and disabled.

Chapultepec. On the 11th of September, I received orders to furnish details of men from the company to assist engineer officers in supervising the construction of batteries against Chapultepec. I was placed in charge of Battery No. 1, on the Tacubaya road, against the southern face of the Castle; and Lieutenant McClellan in charge of Battery No. 2, against the southwestern angle. On the night of the 12th, the details were all called in, and I was directed to furnish implements to the different storming parties which were to assault the castle of Chapultepec on the morning of the 13th.[3]

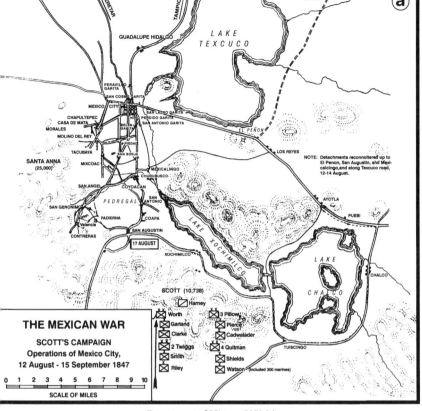

Department of History, USMA

San Cosme Garita. At 3 P.M., that day, I received orders to join the siege train, and report to General Worth whose column was to attack the city by the San Cosme route.

At 4 P.M., I reported to General Worth, who was then with his forces, in the suburbs of the city, on the San Cosme causeway, at the point where it changes direction, at an angle of nearly ninety degrees, and is then nearly straight for about six hundred yards to the fortified Garita in our front. He informed me that Lieutenant Stevens had just been severely wounded and this made me the senior engineer with Worth's division. He directed me to go forward in person, closely examine the condition of affairs at the front, endeavor to determine the best method of operating against the fortified Garita, and report to him the result of my observations as soon as possible. He directed me, particularly, to have in view the question whether it would be advisable to bring the siege guns forward against the embrasured battery at the Garita. Just as I was leaving him, he said: "if you find there are two different methods by which the Garita can be carried, one in a shorter time at a sacrifice of men, the other in longer time, but a saving of men, choose the latter." And he added: "There have been too many valuable lives, of officers and men, lost recently in my division, for nothing."

Though he did not specify the action referred to, he meant the battle of Molino del Rey. Under these instructions, I proceeded to the extreme front, made the requisite examination of our position and that of the enemy, and soon come back. I reported that the houses on the left of the causeway were built up continuously to the battery at the Garita; we could easily break through the walls from house to house; and, under perfect cover, reach the top of a three-story building, with flat roof and stone parapet, within 40 yards of the battery. A fire of musketry from that roof would make the works untenable; and we could thus in a short time drive the enemy from the fortified Garita, and secure a good lodgment within the city, without material loss and without using the siege guns.

General Worth directed me to bring forward the engineer company, which was with the siege train a short distance to the rear, and commence operations on the proposed plan; and at the same time ordered that Clarke's brigade should render any assistance I might call for.

An hour or more before sunset we reached the top of the house above referred to. From that position the inside of the enemy's works could be plainly seen almost to the foot of the interior slope of the parapet. Our first fire upon the Mexicans, who were unconscious of the impending peril, was very deadly. Those who were not killed or disabled by that fire seemed dazed for an instant; but in a few moments, they precipitately retreated, leaving the San Cosme Garita without a single defender in the works. One of their pieces of Artillery was withdrawn a few hundred yards, but was then abandoned.

Immediately after that first fire, a portion of the force with me on the roof became engaged with the enemy who appeared on house tops in rear of their battery. We soon drove them from their position. The other portion of our men fell back to the stairs, made their way to the lower story, broke open the thick, heavily barred, strong door, passed into the street, entered the abandoned works, and pursued the enemy. In the meantime, some of our troops from the right of the causeway had come forward and, a very small number of them were slightly in advance of us in reaching the abandoned battery.

Colonel Garland, commander of the first brigade of Worth's division, on the right of the causeway, says, in his official report: "The enemy then took position at the Garita San Cosme, where they were supported by two pieces of artillery which raked the streets with grape and canister. Finding a secure position to the right of the second defense [about 350 yards in front of the Garita], I reorganized the command as it came up; mounted a howitzer on the top of a convent, which, under the direction of Lieutenant [U. S.] Grant,[4] Quartermaster, 4th Infantry, and Lieutenant Lendrum,[5] 3rd Artillery, annoyed the enemy considerably. About this time, report was made to me that considerable progress had been made by the troops on the other side of the street by means of crowbars and pickaxes, working through houses and yards. This caused me to watch closely for the first movement of the enemy indicative of retreat. The moment this was discovered, the 4th Infantry, followed by detachments of the 2nd and 3rd Artillery, under Colonel Belton, rushed up the road, when they entered the work simultaneously with the forces operating to the right and left, Captain McKenzie's storming party slightly in advance." (Ex. Doc. No. 1, Appendix, p. 170.)

Referring to this operation, General Worth, in his official report, says: "the moment had now arrived for the final and combined attack upon the last stronghold of the enemy in my quarter; it was made, by our men springing, as if by magic, to the tops of the houses into which they had patiently and quietly made their way with the bar and pick, and to the utter surprise and consternation of the enemy, opening upon him, within easy range, a destructive fire of musketry. A single discharge, in which many of his gunners were killed at their pieces, was sufficient to drive him in confusion from the breastworks; when a prolonged shout from our brave fellows announced that we were in possession of the Garita of San Cosme, and already in the city of Mexico." (Ex. Doc. No. 1, p. 392.)

The American army having thus captured the fortifications of the capital of the enemy's country, a magnificent city of nearly 200,000 inhabitants, a secure lodgment was immediately effected in large houses, on the left of the street, a few hundred yards from the Garita. I then proceeded, with the engineer company and an infantry detachment, several hundred yards farther; and found a strong position, on the right of the street where the troops could rest protected from fire. Going farther to the front, I discovered that, 150 yards in advance there was a large convent, on the left of the street, occupied by a strong force. The next cross street, the Paseo, had batteries upon it. These facts were reported to General Worth, who ordered forward two brigades—one to occupy each of the positions selected—and, directed me to place those troops, station the picket-guards, and then, with Lieutenant McClellan, report at his headquarters, which was several hundred yards within the Garita.

The aqueduct, in the middle of the street along which we advanced, was an open stone trough, supported at a height of ten feet, or more, by pillars and arches. There was a good deal of firing down the street from Mexican detachments; but, by taking shelter under the arches, between the pillars, our men, in small groups, were quite well protected. A little before dark, whilst I was under one of the arches at the extreme front, endeavoring to get a closer view of the enemy at the convent and on the Paseo, I was joined by Lieutenant Sydney Smith, of the Fourth Infantry, who had borne several messages from me to General Worth during the afternoon. In a few moments after he joined me we heard horses feet rapidly approaching us from the direction of the citadel. These horsemen were captured, and proved to be three Mexican officers, one of whom was Adjutant-General on the staff of Santa Anna.

Accompanied by Lieutenant McClellan, I reported to General Worth at 10 P.M., and was ordered by him to suspend operations for the night and resume them at daylight. He received us both very kindly, expressed satisfaction with the manner in which the works at the Garita had been carried, and approved of all the dispositions that had been subsequently made of the troops at the front. I called his attention again to the convent, told him that the large Mexican force in that position might give us a great deal of trouble next morning, and asked him to permit me, with the engineer company supported by a detachment of about five hundred men, to pass the convent that night, get into a strong position beyond it, and thus induce the enemy to abandon that position before morning; and said I thought it probable a detachment of five hundred men could reach the main plaza of the city, that night, without material difficulty; and that, in case this force encountered serious opposition, they could take possession of some one of the many large, strong buildings on the way, and hold their own against the whole Mexican army until relief could reach them.

General Worth not only refused to comply with my request; but, ordered both myself and Lieutenant McClellan to remain at his headquarters until 3 A.M., at which hour he said he would have us called, and we could then go to the front and resume our duties.

That arrangement left the engineer company, for the night, at the extreme front, without an officer. In spite of my earnest remonstrances General Worth insisted that we should remain. On the latter point he was inexorable. I finally asked him if I was under arrest. He said "No" and added: "You soon will be if you show further hesitation in obeying my order for you to remain here."

Being awakened by one of General Worth's aides, I asked if it was already 3 o'clock. It seemed to me that I had not been asleep five minutes. The aide said: "It is about 1 o'clock. A deputation from the civil authorities has just informed General Worth that Santa Anna's army evacuated the city before midnight, and they offered to surrender the city. They have been passed on to General Scott, at Tacubaya; and General Worth wishes to see you at once."

The latter told me more fully about the deputation and their proposal to surrender; expressed some doubt in reference to the evacuation of the city by the Mexican army; directed me to return to the front; take the engineer company and a detachment of infantry;

proceed carefully forward, using every precaution; and report to him the slightest indication that the city had not been evacuated. I was directed to examine closely every large building and strong position along our route; and not pass them until thoroughly satisfied that they were not occupied by Mexican soldiers.

This forward movement commenced about 2 A.M. There was some delay in determining whether the strong convent, mentioned above, had been evacuated. Accounts on that subject were conflicting; but a thorough examination of the whole position showed that it was abandoned. I reported that fact to General Worth, and informed him that we would move on with great care, in strict compliance with his instructions.

All buildings of importance were broken open. None of them were occupied by the enemy. From time to time, I reported these facts to General Worth; and, at daylight, I informed him that, from a church steeple near the Alameda, I could see that the Citadel, which had stopped the advance of General Quitman's troops early in the afternoon of the 13th, was deserted. At that time, Lieutenant McClellan reported to me there were no signs of the enemy in any portion of the Alameda; and I suggested to General Worth that his whole division be moved forward.

In the meantime, with the engineer company and the infantry detachment, I passed beyond the Alameda, breaking open, as before, and examining all strong buildings on our route. We had gone more than two blocks in advance of the Alameda, and were closely approaching the Main Plaza and the National Palace, when I received a positive order to countermarch my command, and report to General Worth at the Alameda. I demurred, and told the aide, who bore the order, that I had obeyed all of General Worth's cautionary instructions; that there was no enemy in our front, and no reason for calling us back. The aide replied: "The order is positive. You must go back." I then gave the order to countermarch. On our way, the aide, who was a classmate and intimate friend of mine, said to me; "General Worth is very cross, he is angry. My opinion is that he has received orders from the headquarters of the army which have riled him up badly."

A few days later I learned from General Worth that he received a peremptory order from General Scott not to permit any one under his command to pass beyond the Alameda, until further instructions were received from the General-in-Chief.

For several hours after the engineer company took its place on the right of Worth's division, at the Alameda; all seemed to be quiet in the city. General Quitman's troops, from the Belen Gate, had passed the abandoned citadel, reached the Main Plaza, and took possession of the National Palace. Later, General Scott, with his staff officers and mounted escort, entered the city.

About that time a shot was fired, evidently aimed at General Worth, from a narrow street or lane, opposite the head of the division. The shot missed Worth, but very severely wounded Colonel Garland. General Worth immediately ordered me to take the engineer company, go into the lane, find the man who fired the shot, and hang him.

Within fifty yards we found the man who I believed fired the shot, a rope was placed around his neck, but I did not order my men to hang him. I had no *positive* proof against him. I took the man to General Worth, reported the circumstances of the case, in full; stated the reasons for my belief that the prisoner fired the shot which severely wounded Colonel Garland; and added: "In the absence of specific proof against this man I have brought him to you, and await your further instructions."

To which General Worth replied, in a cold and haughty manner: "This is not the way in which my orders are obeyed by officers of *my division.*"

Colonel Duncan,[6] who was close beside General Worth, both mounted, whilst I was on foot, said, at once, before I could make any reply to the foregoing censure: "General Worth, you are wrong; Lieutenant Smith is right. Under the circumstances he ought not to have hanged this man. It is for you, the Major-General commanding these forces, to decide that matter. Give the order. You see he and his men are ready to obey you. Give the order."

In the meantime, the men of the engineer company, without instructions from me, had passed the rope over an adjacent large lantern iron; and stood ready to string the man up. General Worth did not give the order. The man was not hanged.

In less than an hour after Colonel Garland was wounded, lawless bands of armed Mexicans commenced firing from the parapet roofs of houses, from church steeples and windows, in various parts of the city, upon our troops in the open streets. An order was then given, by General Scott, for Worth's forces to move beyond the Alameda and join with the rest of the army, in putting down the rising of armed outlaws who made this murderous attack upon us eight or ten hours after the city surrendered. In these operations the engineer company was with Worth's division until the recall was sounded late that afternoon.

General Scott, in his official report, says: "I communicated, about daylight [on the 14th], orders to Worth and Quitman to advance slowly and cautiously [to guard against treachery] towards the heart of the city, and to occupy its stronger and more commanding points. Quitman proceeded to the great plaza or square, planted guards and hoisted the colors of the United States on the national palace, containing the halls of Congress and executive apartments of Federal Mexico. In this grateful service, Quitman might have been anticipated by Worth, but for my express orders halting the latter at the head of the *Alameda*, [a green park] within three squares of that goal of general ambition." (Ex. Doc. No. 1, p. 383.)

General Worth, in his official report, says: "At 5 A.M., on the 14th, my troops and heavy guns advanced into the city, and occupied the Alameda to the point where it fronts the palace, and there halted at 6 o'clock, the general-in-chief having instructed me to take a position and await his further orders. Shortly afterwards a straggling assassin-like fire commenced from the house-tops, which continued, in various parts of the city through the day, causing us some loss. The first shot, fired at a group of officers at the head of my column, struck down Colonel Garland, badly wounded. About the time of our entrance into the city, the convicts in the different prisons, to the number of some thirty thousand men, were liberated by order of the flying government, armed and distributed in the most advantageous houses, including the churches, convents, and even the hospitals, for the purpose of exciting, if possible, the city to revolt."

In speaking of the general operations of the forces in the capture of the city, General Worth adds:

"Officers and men of every corps carried themselves with wonted gallantry and conduct. Of the staff; Lieutenants Stevens, Smith, and McClellan, engineers, displayed the gallantry, skill and conduct, which so eminently distinguished their corps." (Ex. Doc. No. 1, pp. 393–4.)

General Scott adds: "Captain Lee, engineer, so constantly distinguished, also bore important orders from me [September 13] until he fainted from a wound and the loss of two nights' sleep at the batteries. Lieutenants Beauregard, Stevens, and Tower, all wounded, were employed with the divisions, and Lieutenants G. W. Smith and G. B. McClellan with the company of sappers and miners. Those five lieutenants of engineers, like their captain, won the admiration of all about them." (Ex. Doc. No. 1, p. 385.)

Major John L. Smith, senior engineer, says: "Lieutenant Smith reports all the sappers who were engaged on the 13th and 14th, to have conducted themselves with intelligence and intrepidity altogether satisfactory; but, he mentions the orderly sergeant, Hastings, who was wounded, as being eminently distinguished, and he mentions also artificer Gerber, as having been particularly distinguished." (Ex. Doc. No. 1, p. 430.)

Without dwelling upon details of the fighting in the streets and houses on the 14th, it may be stated that a short time before the recall was sounded, when Orderly Sergeant Hastings fell, Lieutenant McClellan seized the Sergeant's musket, fired at, and killed the man who shot Hastings. In a few moments thereafter the company passed the dead body of that "liberated," *convict* Mexican.

The unoccupied private house in which we were quartered that night was near the place at which the man, who shot Colonel Garland, had been left tied to a lantern iron with a rope around his neck. When we returned the man was gone. Nothing further was said or done upon our side, in this case.

An hour or more after we were comfortably "settled in our new home," I noticed that McClellan was very quiet for a considerable time, evidently thinking of matters which deeply interested him. An occasional marked change seemed to come over the spirit of his dream. Finally I awakened him from his reverie, saying: "A penny for your thoughts. I have been watching you for half an hour or more, and would like much to know, honor bright, what you have been thinking about."

To which he replied: "I have been making a 'general review' of what we have gone through since we left West Point, one year ago this month, bound for the 'Halls of the Montezumas'; have been again on the Rio Grande, that grave-yard of our forces; have gone over the road from Matamoros to Victoria and Tampico, where we had so much hard work; went through the siege of Vera Cruz, where we were left out in the cold during the ceremonies of surrender, and later, had to make our way as best we could, with the engineer train through the horrid sand; glanced at Cerro Gordo, where it was my misfortune to be with General Pillow's 'whipped community'; stopped again with our friends, the Monks, in the convent at Puebla; crossed over the mountains; came by way of San Antonio, Contreras, Churubusco, Chapultepec and the San Cosme Garita, into this city. Here we are—the deed is done—I am glad no one can say 'poor Mac' over me."

The capture of the city, and its occupation by General Scott's army, virtually ended the war made by the United States against Mexico.[7]

6

In the City of Mexico, Return to West Point

After the street fighting on the 14th, the city was quiet and re-mained so. The men of the company were fairly entitled to a good rest and a new outfit of clothing; but the quartermaster could not then furnish the latter. At their request, I authorized them to purchase a better quality of cloth than that furnished by the government, and to have finer material for trimmings than the coarse cotton braid allowed by the regulations. The clothing was made by good tailors and paid for by the men. In the course of a month or six weeks, the company was provided with handsome, well-fitting uniforms.

In the meantime, drills were suspended for about a month. During that period the only duty required of the men, other than that of ordinary guard over their quarters and the engineer train of the army, was that of details to assist engineer officers in making surveys of the recent battle-fields.

In the latter part of October, the surveys of the battle-fields being completed, and the men provided with new and well-fitting uniforms, infantry drills were resumed. An order was issued requiring the company to be formed without arms, the next day, in the Alameda, for squad drill. Immediately thereafter, one of my most trusted sergeants informed me that this order caused great dissatisfaction in the company. He said the men felt they would be degraded if now turned back to the beginning—at squad drill without arms—thus placing them in the position of raw recruits, whilst the rest of the army were being exercised at brigade and division drill, "evolutions of the line," with all attendant "pomp and circumstance."

The sergeant warned me that the state of feeling in the company would, in his opinion, lead to serious trouble if the order was carried into effect. I thanked him for the information.

When the men were formed on the drill ground next day, I told them I was aware of their opposition to the order; but, that I was under the impression I commanded that company, and if there was a man amongst them who felt disposed to dispute my legal authority he was requested to step to the front. No one moved. I then directed the artificers and privates to go to their quarters, and inform the sergeant of the guard they had my permission to be absent until evening parade. Turning to the non-commissioned officers, I stated that, in my judgment, there was no occasion for them to feel degraded if drilled by their own officers at squad drill without arms.

I drilled the sergeants, McClellan the corporals. Whilst the non-commissioned officers were being thus drilled, the men were allowed daily liberty from quarters. Later, the non-commissioned officers drilled the men in squads under the supervision of the officers. Instruction and practice in the infantry "School of the Company" was then resumed; and, after a time, each non-commissioned officer was required, in turn, to take his place by my side and drill the company. On those occasions, the men were warned that no inattention or remissness on their part would be tolerated; no matter how lenient with them I might choose to be when commanding in person.

It is safe to say that within six weeks from the time squad drills without arms were commenced in the engineer company, in the City of Mexico, that company as Infantry was better drilled than any other in the army. In that respect, and in discipline, they were pattern soldiers. Regular instruction in the "School of the Engineer Soldier" was then resumed.

From raw recruits on the Rio Grande disturbed by the epithet "pick and shovel brigade" applied to them at that time by the soldiers of the line, the engineer company had become veterans of more than half a dozen important battles; had always been in the front of the fighting; and had often been called upon to direct large working parties of soldiers, detailed to use the "pick and shovel."

About two months after we entered the City of Mexico, it was reported to me, by the sergeant of the guard, that Artificer Gerber was then absent, two hours beyond the time limit of his pass. I directed the sergeant to send Gerber to me, in my quarters, as soon as he returned.

Frederick W. Gerber was one of the four men, enlisted by Captain Swift, who had served in the old regular army. He was enlisted as musician, and was the finest bugler in the service. He was soon made company clerk, and had thorough knowledge of routine "company papers." He was German by birth. As company clerk his duties brought him in close relations with the commander of the company; and I soon formed a very high estimate of his qualities as a soldier—and as a man in every respect; except that he would, on occasion, at intervals, when off duty, indulge too freely in strong drink.

I had repeatedly threatened to deprive him of his warrant as artificer, if he did not quit drinking to excess; but I was reluctant to do so, especially because his promotion to that grade was in reward for distinguished gallantry in the attack on the "key-point" of the Mexican position at the battle of Cerro Gordo.

When it was reported to me that he had not returned within the time of his "pass," I was quite sure he was again "on a spree." It was several hours later when he reported to me as ordered by the sergeant of the guard.

I was alone when he entered my room. He had evidently been drinking to excess; but was to some extent recovering. I charged him with being drunk; told him he had behaved so well in that respect lately that I had made up my mind to recommend his being promoted to the grade of corporal; and even to that of sergeant, when opportunity was afforded me, and added: "You know I cannot make such recommendation whilst you continue this habit of getting drunk." He replied: "The lieutenant is mistaken; I am not drunk, and, if he will allow me, I will satisfy him on that point; and explain to him how I happened to overstay my pass." I told him to go on with his explanation.

He said that soon after he left the company quarters, early that morning, with permission to be absent for four hours, he met with a sergeant he had known as a private in the old regular service long before the war. They were glad to see each other, took a few drinks, and then hired a carriage for a drive of several hours in the great city they had helped to capture. He added: "During the drive the sergeant got mad and threatened to have me arrested. I told him that 'no D——d infantry sergeant had rank enough to arrest an artificer of engineers.' He then offered to fight me. We stopped the carriage, got out, drew our swords, and I told him to come on, and we would soon settle the matter. He attacked me, and I disarmed him, kept his sword, made him get into the carriage, drove to General Twiggs's headquarters, reported to the sergeant of his guard, told him what had occurred; and asked him to hold, as a prisoner, the sergeant that had attacked me.

"But he, being also an infantry sergeant, released the sergeant I had brought there, made me a prisoner, and demanded my sword. I gave it to him; but, when he ordered me to give up the sword I had captured, I told him I would see him d——d first; and I kept it. I then asked to be taken before General Twiggs. They told me he was out.

"In three or four hours General Twiggs returned, and when he was passing through the sally-port, the guard all in line, at present-arms, saluting him; I rushed in front of his horse, and calling him by name, told him his guard had made me a prisoner, and I asked for justice at his hands. He ordered me to get out of his way. Still standing in front of his horse, I again asked for justice. To which he replied: 'Who in the h——ll are you?' When I told him who I was, he said: 'How is it that you are a prisoner in my guard-house?' I told General Twiggs the whole story: and showed him the infantry Sergeant's sword I had captured; and which his guard tried to make me give up. General Twiggs then asked me if I was willing to hand that sword to him. I gave it to him at once; and he ordered the sergeant of the guard to release me and give me back my own sword. I then came straight home."

After hearing Gerber's story, on which I placed implicit reliance, I strongly advised him to let liquor alone in future: and, again told him I would gladly have him promoted, if he would quit drinking.

Some time after we returned to the United States, and I had left the company, I learned that, during the time Gerber was closeted with me, opinion in the company was divided, and ran high in regard to the course I would take in his case. All the men knew that he was deservedly a great favorite of mine. Some of them said I would let him off; others that I would deprive him of his warrant as artificer, and otherwise punish him.

These conflicting opinions as to what I would do in Gerber's case, were freely backed by heavy bets among the men. When he joined them, all were anxious to know what "the lieutenant" was going to do—" what did he say?" To which he replied: "It is none of your business." For some time they could get nothing more from him. But he finally said: "D———n it, if you must know; the lieutenant told me he would make me a corporal."

The sergeant who gave me the facts just related, added: "Previous to that time, Gerber was believed, by the whole company, to be a perfectly truthful man. But many of the men thought he lied on that occasion. Although he has been truthful ever since, there is still, amongst us, very grave suspicion in regard to the correctness of his assertion that you then told him you would make him a corporal. I would like very much to know the truth in regard to that matter." I replied: "Gerber told the truth."

It will be shown later, by extracts from official correspondence, that I was not permitted to recommend for promotion, in the company, any of the gallant men under my command who were so highly distinguished in the various battles that occurred in the Valley of Mexico. So I had no opportunity to have Gerber made a corporal—much less a sergeant.[1]

The following extracts from correspondence, and from my monthly reports, give a brief official account of the affairs of the company after the capture of the City of Mexico.

On the 4th of October, 1847, I addressed to Lieutenant I. I. Stevens,[2] Adjutant of Engineers, for the information of the senior engineer in the field, and the General in Chief, a letter from which the following quotations are taken:

"By the last advices that I have received I learn that only six engineer recruits have been made in the United States since September,

1846. During that time the effective strength of the company in the field has been reduced from seventy-one to thirty-six. Something must be done. I have endeavored to reenlist good men whose terms of enlistment in other corps had expired; I have tried to get transfers of good men, and succeeded in obtaining but one. The senior engineer, believing that more could be done, attempted it himself—he procured none.

"At Vera Cruz my men were worked too hard; many of them are suffering yet from disease contracted there. Time, labor and life would have been saved if we had had the proportion of engineer soldiers usual in the armies of civilized nations. At Cerro Gordo, when I could furnish ten men [for details], fifty, at least, were necessary. In the operations in this valley, the same necessity has been felt for a larger number of soldiers of this character. There ought to be more companies of engineer soldiers in this army. Certainly, measures should be taken to complete the number of men allowed in the only company now authorized. I know of none so likely to succeed as sending an officer and non-commissioned officers [to the United States] on this duty."

In my official report for the month of November, 1847, it is stated: "The system of instruction now being pursued is the following: From 9 A.M. until 10:45 A.M., recitations and instruction of the whole company, under direction of both officers, in *Manuel du Sapeur* {the Manual of the Sapper}, together with lectures and recitations on field fortifications. From 11 A.M. until 12:30 P.M. [infantry drill]. From 2 P.M. until 4 P.M., recitations in arithmetic and practice in writing. Each officer has a section in arithmetic, and gives a general superintendence to a section in writing. Instruction in writing is given by sergeants.

"I have nothing new to offer either in reference to the property, the enlistment of men, or the settlement of the accounts of the late Captain Swift. All, in my opinion, {are} matters of importance; but already referred to [in previous reports and correspondence], perhaps, too often.

"It is just one year since, by the casualties of service, the command of this company devolved upon myself as the senior officer for duty with the engineer troops. During this time the interests of the general engineer service, particularly of the non-commissioned officers and men, have materially suffered for want of an officer of rank at the head of the company. In the French service *two* captains are assigned to every company of this character, and the companies are all [well] instructed before they take the field. I earnestly recommend that four officers of engineers be assigned to duty with this company. The commander should be an officer of rank; his position permanent. In case the Chief Engineer should order an officer into the field to take command of Company A, engineers, I respectfully request that I may be ordered to the United States as soon as relieved from this duty."

On the 1st of February, 1848, I reported that the course of instruction, adopted for the company, "had been continued, with satisfactory progress on the part of non-commissioned officers and men."

On the 27th of February, 1848, in a letter to Colonel Totten, Chief Engineer, Washington, D.C., transmitting copies of certain papers, I stated:

"I would respectfully refer you to my communication of October 4th, 1847, addressed to the then Adjutant of Engineers, in which I strongly urged that the interest of the engineer service required that an officer and non-commissioned officers should be ordered to the United States for the purpose of obtaining recruits for this company. Such is the course pursued in every other arm of service: and I hesitate not to say that, had my recommendation, as commander of the engineer company, been acted upon favorably, at that time, we would now have in this city, a full company. I have referred often to the wants of the company, without favorable action having been had on my recommendations. We are not furnished with men, not allowed to take the usual and, in my opinion, necessary means of procuring recruits. I respectfully request to be relieved from the command of the engineer company without further delay than is necessary for the arrival of the captain commander in this city."

Owing to casualties of service, I had almost continually commanded the company, its train, and the general engineer train of the army for more than a year. My rank was that of Second Lieutenant—low on that list. I was conscious that my rank or *lack* of rank, rather, was, in some essential respects, a detriment to the company.

It was believed that the war was over; but, in freely expressing willingness to give up the command I had long exercised, to which I had no claim based upon rank, I did not hesitate to say that: "If the war should be continued, and an additional company of engineer soldiers was authorized to be raised, thus creating an engineer battalion, I would be more than willing to command it in the field: *provided*, I was made Major, by brevet, and assigned to duty with that rank."

In my official report for the month of March, 1848, it is stated: "During the month, daily instruction [of the company] in branches pertaining to engineering has been omitted, I have thought it best to pay more attention to their improvement in writing and arithmetic. The infantry exercises are continued."

On the 1st of May, I reported: "During the month of April the course of instruction and drill pursued in March has been continued, with satisfactory results."

"Three *privates* of this company have been appointed [by the government at Washington] commissioned officers. Three *sergeants*, all men of intelligence, education and character, have been recommended [by me], in compliance with law, for commissions; they having all been repeatedly distinguished for gallant and high soldierly conduct in battle. [As yet] none of these sergeants have received [appointments]."

When it became generally known in the army that the Mexican Government had agreed to the proposed treaty of peace,[3] and that the formal ratification would soon be consummated, I requested the senior engineer, Captain R. E. Lee, to direct me to sell the tools, etc., of the engineer train, in the city of Mexico: order me to proceed to the coast by the first opportunity, for the purpose of looking up, and accounting for, a large amount of engineer property for which the estate of the late Captain A. J. Swift was responsible; and authorize me to turn over the command of the engineer company to Lieutenant McClellan, when I started for the coast.

In compliance with Captain Lee's instructions, the tools were sold. They brought more than they had originally cost in the United States.

I left the city of Mexico the day the treaty of peace was signed on the part of the Mexicans and accompanied General Persifor F. Smith to Vera Cruz, at which place he was charged with making all preparations for the transportation of the army to the United States. Before leaving the City of Mexico I turned over the command of the engineer company to Lieutenant McClellan. I was detained in Vera Cruz about two weeks, obtaining information in regard to, and making disposition of, the public property in that vicinity, for which Captain Swift's estate was then held responsible.

The accounting officers of the government in Washington had charged against him, on their books, the value of large amounts of property which had been shipped to, but never received by him. Several vessels, partly loaded with portions of that property, were shipwrecked by northers {storms} during the siege of Vera Cruz. In the time I spent at that place after the war ended, I obtained knowledge which enabled me to clear up all accounts against the estate of Captain Swift. The amount of that nominal indebtedness far exceeded the value of his property; which would have been unfairly sacrificed to the government, and have left his name unjustly tarnished as that of a defaulter, if conclusive evidence of the facts in the case had not been furnished to the accounting officers.

The engineer company, under Lieutenant McClellan, accompanied by all the engineer officers from the City of Mexico, left that city on the 28th of May, 1848, and marched to Vera Cruz. From the latter place the company was transported by steamer to New York City; arrived at West Point, N.Y., on the 22nd of June; reported to the superintendent of the Military Academy, and was immediately ordered to report to Captain George W. Cullum,[4] of the engineer corps, as its new commander. I remained about a week in Vera Cruz after the company sailed; arrived at West Point in July; and was ordered to report to Captain Cullum.

A short time thereafter, I asked to be relieved from duty with the company; and applied for six months leave of absence. The leave was granted, and it was understood that, on its expiration, I would be ordered to other engineer service.

Before the expiration of my leave, the war men {combat veterans} of the company procured the passage of an act by Congress, authorizing their discharge from the service. Under that act nearly all the men of the company who had served in Mexico immediately obtained their discharge from the army. This virtually reduced the company to the detachment of recruits which had been collected and retained at West Point.

At the expiration of my leave of absence I was formally relieved from further direct service with the engineer company; and at the request of the Chief Engineer, consented to undertake the enlistment of new recruits to fill the places in the company vacated by the war men, who had been discharged. That business was finished within a few months. I was then ordered on other engineer duty and, thus, my connection with the engineer company ended.

Appendix A
Brief Extracts from Wilcox's
History of the Mexican War (1892)

"General Patterson was ordered to march [December, 1846,] from Matamoros to Victoria with three regiments of volunteers, two pieces of artillery, and the engineer company under Lieut. G. W. Smith" (p. 187).

Vera Cruz. "This line of investment, through the chapparal and over the sand hills, was located by Lieut. G. W. Smith, of the engineers, assisted by Lieut. G. B. McClellan, and a roadway along the line was made under the supervision of these two lieutenants with the engineer company and a party of several hundred soldiers" (p. 246).

Cerro Gordo. "On the arrival of the engineer company and train at Plan del Rio [April 17th, 1847], Lieut. G. B. McClellan with a party of ten men reported to General Pillow, and, Lieut. G. W. Smith with [the rest of] his men and a portion of the train to General Twiggs.

"That night [17th] one 24-pounder and two 24-pound howitzers were placed in position on the Atalaya, the battery being constructed under the supervision of Lieut. G. W. Smith, assisted by Lieut. John G. Foster of the engineers, the location of the battery having been determined by Capt. R. E. Lee" (p. 286).

From Puebla to the Valley of Mexico. "Riley's brigade was guided by Capt. Lee, assisted by Lieut. John G. Foster with ten men of the engineer company" (pp. 287–88).

"It was the rule with General Scott that one of the only two regular divisions should always be in front. The engineer company headed the column. There was but one company of engineer soldiers in the United States army" (p. 339).

In the Valley of Mexico. "Beyond San Gregorio, the border of Xochimilco was skirted, and here obstructions in the road were first encountered, a ditch having been dug across it, and large stones rolled down from the hillside; but these obstacles were soon overcome by the engineer company with a detail from the leading brigade, while the Mexicans, who were firing from the heights above, were driven off by Colonel C. F. Smith's light battalion" (p. 355).

Contreras. "The engineer company was recalled from Worth, and with a working party of 500 men, was ordered to make the road to Padierna practicable for artillery" (p. 362).

"When Smith's brigade advanced as described, the engineer company, under Lieut. G. W. Smith, went into action with the Third Infantry of that brigade" (p. 363).

"General Smith moved to his right and front across the *pedrigal*, the Rifles, with the engineer company at their head, leading."

"At 2:30 A.M. of the 20th [August, 1847], the troops under General Smith began to form and take their places preparatory to the march which would bring them on Valencia's rear. Leading the Rifles in front of the brigade was the engineer company" (p. 369).

"The engineer company and the Rifles, being already in position in rear of the Mexican detachment, then rose and firing a volley upon it, and Bennet Riley continuing on upon them, they faced about, broke, and fled in the utmost precipitation to the main line in rear, pursued by Riley, the Rifles and engineer company" (p. 70).

Churubusco. "At Coyacan General Scott joined, having previously ordered his columns to halt there. Lieut. I. I. Stevens, ordered about the same time to advance on the direct road and reconnoitre, was supported by the engineer company under Lieut. G. W. Smith. This reconnaissance covered the Convent of San Pablo in the village of Churubusco" (pp. 378–89).

Chapultepec. "Battery No. 1 was constructed under Lieut. G. W. Smith's supervision, and Battery No. 2 under Lieut. G. B. McClellan's.

Details were made from Quitman's division to assist the engineer company in the construction of these works, but although directed to report immediately after dark they did not arrive until near 4 A.M., of the 12th; hence these works, which were to have been finished before daylight, were hardly commenced by that time. The engineers were however, indefatigable, and the batteries were completed rapidly" (p. 452).

City of Mexico. "Lieut. G. W. Smith, with the company and train under his command, reported to General Worth on the [San Cosme] causeway, [in the afternoon, September 13th], was informed that the wounding of Lieut. Stevens made him [Smith] the senior engineer of the attack then going on, and was instructed to go to the front, closely and carefully examine the state of affairs, return as soon as practicable, and report the best method of conducting the attack." He reported "that infantry alone on the left of the road could capture the gate, without artillery and with little loss, by making its way through the houses. He was ordered to take the engineer company and tools, return to the front, and carry out the plan proposed" (p. 476).

"The Mexicans did not remain long in front of Worth; after dark the signal for retreat of one command was given, and being heard by all, they left the buildings and scattered in all directions, their officers being unable to restrain them. In a little while, however, they repaired to the citadel. In one of the pavilions a council was held. Santa Anna presided, explained the untoward incidents of the day, and asked the opinions of those present as to whether or not the defence of the capital should be prolonged. There was discussion and opposition, but, Santa Anna announced his decision in these emphatic words: 'I resolve that this night this city must be evacuated'" (pp. 480–81).

"At 1 o'clock A.M. of the 14th commissioners from the municipal government of the city approached the advanced post of Worth's command, were passed to his headquarters, and by him sent to General Scott's headquarters in Tacubaya" (p. 481).

"General Worth then directed the two engineer officers, serving with his command, to proceed to the front and with a detachment of infantry and the engineer company, closely examine all strong buildings, and direct operations toward the Main Plaza and National Palace. The senior engineer being directed to make known promptly any indication that the rumored evacuation was incorrect, reported that everything indicated that the Mexican army had abandoned the city" (p. 481).

Appendix B
Promotions of Enlisted Men of
the Company

Tepe Agualco, Mexico,
May 4, 1847

Colonel JOSEPH G. TOTTEN,
Chief Engineer,
Washington City

Sir:

I have the honor to inform you that, on the 25th of April, First Sergeant Hastings of "K" Company, Third Artillery, was, by order of General Worth, transferred to the Engineer Corps, subject to the approval of the Commander-in-Chief.

Sergeant Hastings has the reputation of being one of the best first sergeants in the army. He was for 7 or 8 years orderly sergeant in the Second Infantry. He is an intimate friend of Sergeant Everett;[1] is a well educated man, very intelligent; a remarkable fine looking soldier, a good drill sergeant.

By birth he is an Irishman—he came to this country quite young, and was brought up in Po'keepsie, N.Y.

We were very much in want of an orderly sergeant. I think there can be no doubt but we have secured a prize.

I would be glad if you would send a Sergeant's warrant for David H. Hastings. I respectfully recommend the following promotions and appointments in the engineer company:

Corporal Benjamin W. Coit, acting lance sergeant since 1st of February, to be sergeant from February 1st, 1847:

Artificer Charles A. Viregg, lance corporal since 1st of February, to be corporal from February 1st, 1847:

Artificer Ethan T. Sheldon, lance corporal since 1st of February, to be corporal from February 1st, 1847:

Artificer William A. Noyes, to be corporal from the 18th of April, 1847;

Privates Charles A. Pierce, Jacob T. Smith, Benjamin L. Boomer, Edwin M. Holloway, James Brannan, Joseph A. Mower, David P. Weaver, Thomas Bigley, Seth H. Taylor, and Charles A. Porter, to be artificers from the 29th of March, 1847:

Musician Frederick W. Gerber to be artificer from the 18th of April, 1847:

Privates Augustus B. Hussey, James B. Vansant, and William S. Bliss, to be artificers from the 29th of March, 1847:

Corporal William Bartlett, reduced to the grade of artificer, May 1st, 1847:

Artificer Hiram B. Yeager to be corporal from May 1st, 1847:

Artificer Charles W. Bont reduced to the grade of second class private from May 1st, 1847.

I respectfully call to the attention of the Chief Engineer the fact that, in accordance with his suggestion, I have delayed making the above recommendations, and now urge them as my deliberate opinion. I hope they will be favorably acted upon.

My monthly return for April shows a total of sixty-two. My recommendations make, in the company, six sergeants, six corporals, one musician, twenty-three artificers and twenty-six second class privates.

Very respectfully,

Your obdt. Servt.,

GUS. W. SMITH,

Lieut., Comdg. Engr. Co.

The foregoing recommendations were approved and the appointments were received whilst the company was in the city of Puebla.

Soon after the war ended, Sergeants Hastings, Starr and Everett were promoted to be commissioned officers in the "Old Regular Army" of the United States. Later, Sergeant Warren L. Lothrop was given a commission in that army.

Notes

Introduction

1. A total of forty-three engineer officers served in the U.S. Army during the Mexican War. Of that number, nineteen served with the Corps of Engineers and twenty-four with the Corps of Topographical Engineers. For an excellent discussion of the duties of engineers, see Theophilus F. Rodenbough, *The Army of the United States: Historical Sketches of Staff and Line with Portraits of Generals-in-Chief* (New York: Maynard, Merrill, 1896), 113–21.

2. George W. Cullum, *Biographical Register of the Officers and Graduates of the U.S. Military Academy at West Point, N.Y.* (Boston: Houghton Mifflin, 1891), 1:448. A detailed obituary of Captain Swift can be found in the *New Orleans Commercial Bulletin,* Apr. 27, 1847.

3. Leonne M. Hudson, *The Odyssey of a Southerner: The Life and Times of Gustavus Woodson Smith* (Macon, Ga.: Mercer Univ. Press, 1998), 1–12.

4. Thomas J. Roland, "George Brinton McClellan (December 3, 1826–October 29, 1885)," in *Leaders of the American Civil War: A Biographical and Historiographical Dictionary,* ed. Charles F. Ritter and Jon L. Wakelyn (Westport, Conn.: Greenwood Press, 1998), 259–70.

5. John C. Waugh, *The Class of 1846, from West Point to Appomattox: Stonewall Jackson, George McClellan and Their Brothers* (New York: Warner Books, 1994), 75–76.

6. Alexander J. Swift to his father, Aug. 16, 1846, Alexander J. Swift Papers, Special Collections and Archives Division, U.S. Military Academy, West Point, N.Y.

7. *New Orleans Commercial Bulletin,* Apr. 27, 1847; see also the *Daily Picayune* (New Orleans), Apr. 25, 1847.

8. The awarding of brevet rank to American soldiers for gallant or meritorious service in wartime was predominantly a nineteenth-century practice. This quasi-honorary title, which the U.S. Army adopted from Great Britain, sometimes created "confusion in terms of precedence and authority." Many soldiers returning home from Mexico did so not only with the memory of a victorious campaign but also with one, two, or three brevets. William B. Skelton maintains that "during the Mexican War especially the pursuit of brevets became an obsession." Trevor N. Dupuy, Curt Johnson, and Grace P. Hayes, comps., *Dictionary of Military Terms: A Guide to the Language of Warfare and Military Institutions* (New York: H. W. Wilson, 1986), 36; William B. Skelton, *An American Profession of Arms: The Army Officer Corps, 1784–1861* (Lawrence: Univ. Press of Kansas, 1992), 195.

9. Hudson, *The Odyssey of a Southerner*, 204–18.

10. Many officers of the old army resigned their commissions during the antebellum period because of the snail's pace of promotions. Among the principal factors that made the prospects of advancement in rank dismal were the extremely slow rate of growth in the army, the small number of retirements, and the seniority system. Detractors of the seniority system blame it for discouraging talented officers and fostering "intellectual stagnation" in the army. In general, soldiers received promotions as a result of retirements, the creation of new regiments, and rank by brevet. Russell F. Weigley, *History of the United States Army* (New York: Macmillan, 1967), 168–69; Skelton, *An American Profession of Arms*, 47–51.

Chapter 1

1. Commissioned officers of the U.S. armed forces received their commissions from the president, who also awarded rank. Noncommissioned officers held rank by appointment, not by commission. It was the responsibility of officers of units to appoint noncommissioned officers. Dupuy, Johnson, and Hayes, *Dictionary of Military Terms*, 159, 162.

2. Zachary Taylor, the twelfth president of the United States, was born on November 24, 1784, in Virginia. He saw action in the War of 1812 and the Black Hawk War and fought Indians in Florida before the start of the Mexican conflict. When General Taylor arrived at Corpus Christi in February 1846, his army totaled nearly four thousand soldiers. Years after the war Ulysses S. Grant reflected on Taylor's force, declaring that "a better army, man for man, probably never faced an enemy than the one commanded by General Taylor in the earliest two engagements of the Mexican War." President Taylor died on July 9, 1850, sixteen months after his inauguration. K. Jack Bauer, *Zachary Taylor: Soldier, Planter, Statesman of the Old Southwest* (1985; reprint, Baton Rouge: Louisiana State Univ. Press, 1993), xxi–2; Weigley, *History of the United States Army*, 173–74.

3. Camargo, a town with a population of three thousand, was situated on the Rio Grande upriver from Matamoros. The scorching heat combined with unsanitary

conditions in the town, surrounded as it was by limestone rock, was a prescription for the spread of maladies among the soldiers. Camargo became a morgue for 1,500 Americans who succumbed to diseases. Seymour V. Connor and Odie B. Faulk, *North America Divided: The Mexican War 1846–1848* (New York: Oxford Univ. Press, 1971), 44.

4. Tampico was one of the most important port cities in Mexico. Located on the Gulf coast, this heavily fortified city had a fascinating past as a sanctuary for numerous revolutions. George E. Meade described Tampico as a "delightful place," possessing "all the luxuries of a somewhat civilized town." John S. D. Eisenhower, *So Far from God: The U.S. War with Mexico 1846–1848* (New York: Random House, 1989), 157–58; George Meade, *The Life and Letters of George Gordon Meade,* ed. George Gordon Meade (New York: Scribner's, 1913), 177.

5. Victoria was the capital city of the Mexican state of Tamaulipas, which was under the military authority of Gen. Gabriel Valencia. That city was occupied by Taylor and Patterson in January 1847.

6. George A. McCall (1802–1868) of Philadelphia graduated from the U.S. Military Academy in 1822. He had fought Seminole Indians in the 1830s. His brilliant leadership of an infantry battalion in the Mexican War earned him two brevets. During the Civil War, he commanded the Pennsylvania Reserve Corps during the Peninsula campaign. When hostilities ended, McCall worked as a farmer in his home state until his passing. Mark Mayo Boatner, *The Civil War Dictionary,* rev. ed. (New York: David Mckay, 1988), 522–23.

7. Robert Patterson, born in Ireland in 1792, came to America with his family after the Irish Rebellion of 1798. The family settled in Pennsylvania. After serving in the War of 1812, he returned to Philadelphia and went into business. Patterson became a veteran of the Mexican War and an entrepreneur, with interests in the sugar and textile industries. He served in the Union army as a major general for three months. General Patterson was mustered out of service in July 1861 and returned to Philadelphia, where he died in 1881. Dumas Malone, *Dictionary of American Biography* (New York: Scribner's, 1936), 14:306–7.

8. David E. Twiggs, "the oldest officer of the old army to take up arms for the Confederacy," was born in Georgia in 1790. A veteran of the War of 1812, he fought Indians on the frontier prior to the Mexican War. His exceptional service in the Mexican War earned him the rank of brevet major general. In 1861, he was commissioned a major general in the Confederate army and ordered to Louisiana to assume command of that district. General Twiggs died in 1862, in the state of his birth. Ezra J. Warner, *Generals in Gray: Lives of the Confederate Commanders* (Baton Rouge: Louisiana State Univ. Press, 1959), 312.

9. John G. Foster (1823–1874) graduated near the top of his West Point class in 1846. A skilled engineer, Foster received two brevets for extraordinary service during the Mexican conflict. He was on duty at Fort Sumter when it came under attack on April 12. General Foster commanded several military departments in

the Union army during the Civil War. Mitchell A. Yockelson, "Foster, John Gray," in *Biographical Dictionary of the Union: Northern Leaders of the Civil War,* eds. John T. Hubbell and James W. Geary (Westport, Conn.: Greenwood Press, 1995), 181–82.

10. One of the best soldiers in the history of the nation, Winfield Scott was born on June 13, 1786, at Laurel Branch, a short distance from Petersburg. He served with distinction in the War of 1812. Though contentious, General Scott led the American forces to victory in the Mexican War. He was the nominee of the Whig party in the presidential election of 1852. The Virginia native was the first general in chief of the U.S. Army; however, ill health forced him to resign that post in October 1861. He died at the U.S. Military Academy in May 1866. Malone, *Dictionary of American Biography,* 18:598–99.

11. William J. Worth (1794–1849) of New York received two brevets for gallantry in the War of 1812. After that conflict, he served eight years as commandant of cadets at West Point. Worth, a proud and quarrelsome officer, distinguished himself for courage during the Mexican War. President James K. Polk made Worth a brevet brigadier general for meritorious service against the Seminole Indians in Florida. Malone, *Dictionary of American Biography,* 20:536–37.

12. At that time, McClellan was about 20 years of age (Smith annotation).

Chapter 2

1. Gideon J. Pillow was born on June 8, 1806, in Williamson, Tennessee. He practiced law in his home state; he also dabbled in politics, but he never gained notoriety in that arena. At the outbreak of the Mexican War, President Polk appointed him a brigadier general of volunteers, in which capacity he saw action in several battles. He also served in the "Provisional Army of the Confederacy" as a brigadier general. As a soldier, General Pillow was arrogant, argumentative, and unsuccessful. He died on October 8, 1878, in Arkansas. Warner, *Generals in Gray,* 214.

2. The following quotations from General Scott's official report illustrate the character of the work done during the first two or three days after the landing: "The environs of the city outside the fire of its guns, and those of the castle, are broken into innumerable hills of loose sand, from twenty to two hundred and fifty feet in height, with almost impassable forest of chapparal between." "In extending the line of investment around the city the troops, for three days have performed the heaviest labors in getting over the hills and cutting through the intervening forests" ("Ex Doc. No. 1" p. 216) (Smith annotation).

3. Robert E. Lee was active in several arenas during the mid-nineteenth century. Born in Virginia on January 19, 1807, he arrived at the West Point campus in 1825; He graduated four years later, second in his class. Lee was a member of General Scott's inner circle, emerging from the Mexican War as a brevet colonel. Prior to the Civil War, he served as the superintendent of West Point, commanded soldiers in Texas, and captured John Brown at Harpers Ferry. General

Lee became the daring and resourceful commander of the Army of Northern Virginia. Lee died at Lexington, Virginia, on October 12, 1870. Leonne M. Hudson, "Robert Edward Lee (January 19, 1807–October 12, 1870)," in *Leaders of the American Civil War,* eds. Ritter and Wakelyn, 221–34.

4. Pierre G. T. Beauregard (1818–1893) of Louisiana graduated from the Military Academy in the class of 1838. Brave and perceptive, he was one of General Scott's most valued engineers during the Mexican War. He flirted with the idea of joining William Walker's filibuster movement against Nicaragua in the 1850s. Beauregard was appointed a brigadier general in the Confederate army in 1861. He died in New Orleans. Herman M. Hattaway and Michael J. C. Taylor, "Pierre Gustave Toutant Beauregard (May 28, 1818–February 20, 1893)," in *Leaders of the American Civil War,* eds. Ritter and Wakelyn, 19–30.

5. The top graduate of the West Point class of 1841 was Zealous B. Tower (1819–1900) of Massachusetts. His distinguished service as an engineer in the Mexican War earned him the brevet rank of major. He displayed extraordinary bravery as a Union officer during the Civil War and was breveted major general in 1865. General Tower passed away in Cohasset, the town of his birth. Robert H. Jones, "Tower, Zealous Bates," in *Biographical Dictionary of the Union,* eds. Hubbell and Geary, 537.

6. According to Lieutenant McClellan, the superiority of American firepower gave Scott's army a significant advantage over the Mexicans at Vera Cruz. See William Starr Myers, ed., *The Mexican War Diary of George B. McClellan* (Princeton, N.J.: Princeton Univ. Press, 1917), 71.

Chapter 3

1. Taken from my official report for the month of April, 1847. G.W.S. (Smith annotation).

2. One of the more fascinating and colorful Mississippi politicians during the antebellum period was John A. Quitman. Born in Rhinebeck, New York, in 1798, he relocated to Natchez in the early 1820s. There he cultivated a career in politics. He was commissioned a brigadier general of volunteers at the start of the Mexican War. One historian describes Quitman as "the most strident slavery imperialist in the entire South" and as "one of the South's most vocal and persistent radicals." General Quitman died at his home in Mississippi in 1858. Malone, *Dictionary of American Biography,* 15:315–16; Robert E. May, *John A. Quitman: Old South Crusader* (Baton Rouge: Louisiana State Univ. Press, 1985), xv–xvi.

3. Colonel Joseph G. Totten, Chief Engineer, had left Vera Cruz and returned to his duties in Washington, D.C. Major John L. Smith then became Senior Engineer with General Scott's forces (Smith annotation).

4. Peter V. Hagner (1815–1893) of Washington, D.C., graduated from West Point in 1836. He was twice breveted for meritorious conduct in the Mexican War. He reached the rank of lieutenant colonel in the Union army in 1863. Boatner, *Civil War Dictionary,* 365.

5. Prior to the outbreak of the Mexican War, Persifor F. Smith (1798–1858) of Philadelphia had graduated from the College of New Jersey, practiced law, fought in the Seminole War, and served as city judge of Jefferson Parish in Louisiana. This intrepid officer was breveted major general for distinguished service at Churubusco, Chapultepec, and the Belen Gate. He died at Fort Leavenworth, Kansas. Malone, *Dictionary of American Biography*, 17:331–32.

6. This disease, also known as yellow fever, was dreaded by the American soldiers at Vera Cruz.

7. Bayonets were among the weapons used at Cerro Gordo on April 19, 1847. According to an American officer, the battlefield was covered with dead and wounded men. With the snow covered peaks of Orizaba as a backdrop to Jalapa, Captain Kirby Smith described the village as "the prettiest town I have seen" in Mexico. Richard Bruce Winders, *Mr. Polk's Army: The American Military Experience in the Mexican War* (College Station: Texas A&M Univ. Press, 1997), 162–63; Eisenhower, *So Far From God*, 295.

Chapter 4

1. The dominant personality in the history of Mexico from its independence from Spain in 1821 to the eve of the Mexican War was Antonio Lopez de Santa Anna. A man of boundless energy and charisma, Santa Anna did not hesitate to exercise the prerogatives of a revolutionary leader. One of his major deficiencies was his lack of formal military training. As a soldier in the Spanish army, however, his courage had been unquestioned. Santa Anna was elected president of Mexico in 1833. Three years later, Texas won its independence from Mexico after defeating Santa Anna's army at the battle of San Jacinto. Santa Anna was deposed, but he regained the presidency of Mexico in 1841 through a coup. He would serve in that position until 1844, when he was permanently removed. Eisenhower, *So Far from God*, 8–16.

2. Charles F. Smith of Philadelphia was born on April 24, 1807. The 1825 West Point graduate emerged from the Mexican War with three brevets. Smith's reputation as an outstanding soldier was well known prior to his enlistment into the Union army. He was promoted to the rank of major general in March 1862 and saw action in the western theater. Smith died on April 25, 1862, in Tennessee. Ezra J. Warner, *Generals in Blue: Lives of the Union Commanders* (Baton Rouge, Louisiana State Univ. Press, 1964), 455–56.

3. John C. Pemberton (1814–1881) of Philadelphia graduated from the U.S. Military Academy in 1837. He was an Indian fighter and veteran of the Mexican War, in which he received two brevets. Pemberton was promoted to the rank of lieutenant general in the Confederate army in October 1862; his Civil War career would be remembered for his surrender of Vicksburg. Jon L. Wakelyn, *Biographical Dictionary of the Confederacy* (Westport, Conn.: Greenwood Press, 1977), 340–41.

4. Santa Anna's army fought courageously at the battles of Contreras and Churubusco in the Valley of Mexico. To facilitate the forward movement of Scott's army,

the engineer company carved a road through the Pedregal, a rugged piece of land that appeared to have been forgotten by time. The Americans attacked the entrenched Mexicans at Contreras on August 19 but failed to dislodge them. The Americans resumed their assault on Gen. Gabriel Valencia's position early in the morning of August 20; this time success crowned their efforts. According to Gen. Persifor Smith, the Mexican army of six thousand troops was routed in seventeen minutes. Waugh, *The Class of 1846*, 105–11.

5. Earl Van Dorn was born in Mississippi in 1820. He graduated from West Point in 1842, fifty-second in a class of fifty-six. He received two brevets for meritorious service in the Mexican War. The Mississippi native joined the Confederacy in 1861, and he was promoted to the rank of major general in September of that year. General Van Dorn was murdered on May 8, 1863, at Spring Hill, Tennessee, by a civilian of that community. Warner, *Generals in Gray*, 314–15.

6. Following their triumph at Contreras, the Americans pursued their adversaries on the road to Churubusco. At the church of Churubusco, the armies fought a ferocious battle. It was not until late in the afternoon that the Americans forced the Mexicans to surrender. When the smoke had cleared from the American victories of August 20, Scott's army was less than five miles from Mexico City. The casualties suffered by Santa Anna's army in the one day of fighting totaled four thousand killed or wounded and three thousand taken prisoner. General Scott did not escape the action of August 20 unscathed. He lost 1,053 men, of whom 139 were killed. Eisenhower, *So Far from God*, 325–27.

Chapter 5

1. The armistice, which became effective on August 24, 1847, raised hopes that an end to the conflict was at hand. Scott, who had established his headquarters at Tacubaya, a picturesque village less than three miles from the Mexican capital, was suspicious of Santa Anna. He believed that the Mexican leader was not serious about reaching a final peace settlement but instead had used the armistice and subsequent negotiations to stall for time to strengthen the fortifications of the capital city. The talks abruptly ended on September 6, with Scott accusing Santa Anna of violating the terms of the agreement. The next day, the U.S. force at Tacubaya prepared for another push toward Mexico City. John Edwards Weems, *To Conquer a Peace: The War between the United States and Mexico* (Garden City, N.Y.: Doubleday, 1974), 410–13.

2. The Molino del Rey was a huge set of buildings located in the western section of the grounds of Chapultepec. Santa Anna, who expected an assault on that place, moved a large force there on September 7, 1847. In a prophetic letter to his wife the night before the battle, Capt. Ephraim Kirby Smith said, "Tomorrow will be a day of slaughter." This was his last letter. With a force of about 3,500 soldiers, General Worth attacked Molino del Rey on September 8. Victory for the United States in

the fierce two-hour battle came at a high price: American casualties totaled almost eight hundred killed, wounded, and missing. General Worth estimated that Santa Anna's army suffered more than two thousand casualties. Robert Seth Henry, *The Story of the Mexican War* (Indianapolis: Bobbs-Merrill, 1950), 351–55.

3. The castle of Chapultepec, which commanded the roads into Mexico City, was the scene of one of the last battles of the war. The lowering of the Mexican flag from the castle by Capt. John G. Barnard on September 13 was symbolic of the enemy's declining resistance.

4. Ulysses S. Grant was born in Ohio in 1822. He entered West Point in 1839, graduating twenty-first in a class of thirty-nine cadets in 1843. Grant served in the Mexican War with Zachary Taylor and Winfield Scott, emerging from that conflict "with a reputation for modesty, competence, and coolness under fire." Joining the Union army a little more than a decade later, Grant would prove indispensable to the war effort of the United States. Ultimately becoming general in chief of the Union armies, he would be instrumental in toppling the Confederacy. The crowning achievement of Grant's political career was his election to the presidency in 1868. John T. Hubbell, "Ulysses Simpson Grant (April 27, 1822–July 25, 1885)," in *Leaders of the American Civil War,* eds. Ritter and Wakelyn, 153–68.

5. Smith is probably referring to Thomas W. Lendrum, who was an artillerist, West Point graduate, and Indian fighter. He died in 1852 in new York City.

6. Shortly after James Duncan's graduation from West Point in 1834, he went to Florida to fight Indians. His gallantry in the Mexican War earned him two brevets. Once the fighting had stopped in the Mexican capital, Duncan and two of his fellow Democratic officers took part in a scheme "to discredit Scott by claiming that the Whig general had little role in the capture of Mexico City." Angered by their allegation, Scott retaliated by arresting the three Democrats. President Polk's intervention in the matter resulted in the release of the arrested officers. Duncan died in Alabama in 1849 at the age of thirty-six. Cullum, *Biographical Register of the Officers and Graduates,* 1:41; Winders, *Mr. Polk's Army,* 189.

7. Mexico City surrendered to the U.S. Army on September 14, 1847.

Chapter 6

1. Frederick W. Gerber, was enlisted in Co. "A" on June 29, 1846, after previous service in the 4th Infantry, which he joined in 1839, and under the act of March 3, 1849, was discharged April 6, 1849. He was reenlisted the same day and continued in the service until his death at the Post of Willets Point, N.Y., on November 10, 1877. He was appointed Artificer on April 18, 1847, Corporal, August 1, 1848, and was Sergeant Major of the Battalion of Engineers from February 21, 1867, to his death (Smith annotation).

2. Iassac I. Stevens, who graduated first in the West Point class of 1839, was born in March 1818 in Massachusetts. After leaving the Military Academy, he worked

for several years as an engineer on fortifications in New England. Stevens, the courageous Adjutant of Engineers received two brevets for meritorious service during the Mexican War. He joined the Union army shortly after the attack on Fort Sumter. He was killed at the battle of Chantilly on September 1, 1862. Warner, *Generals in Blue,* 475–76.

3. President Polk's envoy to Mexico during the war was Nicholas P. Trist, who negotiated the Treaty of Guadalupe Hidalgo. He and the Mexican commissioners signed the treaty on February 2, 1848. Five weeks later, on March 10, the Senate ratified the treaty by a vote of thirty-eight to fourteen. The Treaty of Guadalupe Hidalgo became effective on May 30, when the belligerent countries formally exchanged ratifications.

4. George W. Cullum was born in New York in 1809 but relocated to Pennsylvania at an early age. He was appointed to West Point from the latter state, graduating third in his class of 1833. He was chief of staff to Henry Halleck during the Civil War. In 1890, he published his monumental *Biographical Register of the Officers and Graduates of the United States Military Academy,* which contains a military summary of all the graduates from 1802 to 1899. General Cullum died in New York City in 1892. Boatner, Civil *War Dictionary,* 211–12.

Appendix B

1. Thornton S. Everett was property sergeant of the engineer company; had charge of its train from the time of his enlistment in the company until its return to West Point; and, in addition, had charge, in Mexico, of the general engineer train of the army (Smith annotation).

Bibliography

Manuscript Collection

Swift, Alexander J. Papers. Special Collections and Archives Division, U.S. Military Academy Library, West Point, New York.

Memoirs and Journals

Meade, George. *The Life and Letters of George Gordon Meade*. Edited by George Gordon Meade. 2 vols. New York: Scribner's, 1913.

Myers, William Starr, ed. *The Mexican War Diary of George B. McClellan*. Princeton, N.J.: Princeton Univ. Press, 1917.

Newspapers

New Orleans Daily Picayune 1847.
New Orleans Commercial Bulletin 1847.

Books

Bauer, K. Jack. Zachary Taylor: Soldier, Planter, Statesman of the Old Southwest. 1985. Reprint, Baton Rouge: Louisiana State Univ. Press, 1993.

Boatner, Mark Mayo. *The Civil War Dictionary*. Rev. ed. New York: David Mckay, 1988.

Connor, Seymour V., and Odie B. Faulk. *North America Divided: The Mexican War, 1846–1848*. New York: Oxford Univ. Press, 1971.

Cullum, S. George W. *Biographical Register of the Officers and Graduates of the U.S. Military Academy at West Point, New York.* 3 vols. with supplements. Boston: Houghton Mifflin, 1891.

Dupuy, Trevor N., Curt Johnson, and Grace P. Hayes, comps. *Dictionary of Military Terms: A Guide to the Language of Warfare and Military Institutions.* New York: H. W. Wilson, 1986.

Eisenhower, John S. D. *So Far from God: The U.S. War with Mexico 1846–1848.* New York: Random House, 1989.

Esposito, Vincent J., ed. *The West Point Atlas of American Wars, 1689–1900.* Vol. 1. New York: Praeger, 1959.

Henry, Robert Selph. *The Story of the Mexican War.* Indianapolis: Bobbs-Merrill, 1950.

Hubbell, John T., and James W. Geary. *Biographical Dictionary of the Union: Northern Leaders of the Civil War.* Westport, Conn.: Greenwood Press, 1995.

Hudson, Leonne M. *The Odyssey of a Southerner: The Life and Times of Gustavus Woodson Smith.* Macon, Ga.: Mercer Univ. Press, 1998.

Johnson, Allen, and Dumas Malone. *Dictionary of American Biography.* 20 vols. New York: Scribner's, 1928–44.

May, Robert E. *John A. Quitman: Old South Crusader.* Baton Rouge: Louisiana State Univ. Press, 1985.

Ritter, Charles F., and John L. Wakelyn, eds. Leaders of the American Civil War: A Biographical and Historiographical Dictionary. Westport, Conn.: Greenwood Press, 1998.

Rodenbough, Theophilus F. *The Army of the United States: Historical Sketches of Staff and Line with Portraits of Generals-in-Chief.* New York: Maynard, Merrill, 1896.

Skelton, William B. *An American Profession of Arms: The Army Officer Corps, 1784–1861.* Lawrence: Univ. Press of Kansas, 1992.

Wakelyn, Jon L. *Biographical Dictionary of the Confederacy.* Westport, Conn.: Greenwood Press, 1977.

Warner, Ezra J. *Generals in Blue: Lives of the Union Commanders.* Baton Rouge: Louisiana State Univ. Press, 1964.

———. *Generals in Gray: Lives of the Confederate Commanders.* Baton Rouge: Louisiana State Univ. Press, 1959.

Waugh, John C. *The Class of 1846, from West Point to Appomattox: Stonewall Jackson, George McClellan and Their Brothers.* New York: Warner Books, 1994.

Weems, John Edwards. *To Conquer a Peace: The War between the United States and Mexico.* Garden City, N.Y.: Doubleday, 1974.

Weigley, Russell F. *History of the United States Army.* New York: Macmillan, 1967.

Winders, Richard Bruce. *Mr. Polk's War: The American Military Experience in the Mexican War.* College Station: Texas A&M Univ. Press, 1997).

Index

Company "A" Corps of Engineers, U. S. A., 1846–1848,

in the Mexican War, by Gustavus Woodson Smith

was designed and composed by Christine Brooks

in 11/14 Bembo;

printed on 60# Supple Opaque stock

by Thomson-Shore, Inc., of Dexter, Michigan;

and published by

The Kent State University Press

KENT, OHIO 44242